# SILENT RESOLVE

## and the

## GOD WHO LET ME DOWN

# SILENT RESOLVE

## and the

## GOD WHO LET ME DOWN

### (a 9/11 story)

SUSAN VAN VOLKENBURGH

WestBow
PRESS
A DIVISION OF THOMAS NELSON

Edited by Shelly Hulme and Karen Summerville

Unless otherwise stated, all scripture taken from the New King James Version. Copyright 1979, 1980, 1982 by Thomas Nelson, Inc. Used by permission. All rights reserved.

Where indicated, scripture taken from the Holy Bible, New International Version, NIV. Copyright 1973, 1978, 1984 by International Bible Society. Used by permission of Zondervan. All rights reserved.

Cover image by Ashley Van Volkenburgh
Pentagon Memorial—September 11, 2008

WestBow Press books may be ordered through booksellers or by contacting:

WestBow Press
A Division of Thomas Nelson
1663 Liberty Drive
Bloomington, IN 47403
www.westbowpress.com
1-(866) 928-1240

ISBN: 978-1-4497-4338-3 (hc)
ISBN: 978-1-4497-4337-6 (sc)
ISBN: 978-1-4497-4336-9 (e)

Library of Congress Control Number: 2012904664

Printed in the United States of America

WestBow Press rev. date: 05/17/2012

To my father and all those affected by the tragic
events of September 11

*Songs like trees bear fruit only in their own time
and in their own way: and sometimes they are
withered untimely.*

~ *J. R. R. Tolkien*[1]

# CONTENTS

A special thank you to those who stood by me
during the years following September 11, 2001.
Thank you for the support and encouragement
as I stepped out into the unknown.
To my husband and children
for tolerating the years of emotional upheaval.
To Karen and Valerie for your staunch belief in my writing
and the time spent reviewing my manuscript helping me
become a better writer.

Thank you WestBow Press for providing a medium
in which to deliver my story. Kathy Lester who
guided and encouraged me through the
publishing process.

# PREFACE

So long I have been in writing this book that I hope my words will still hold some resonance upon the reader. I have tried many times to begin, but each time I drew up short. I was not ready. Each time I began, a wave of grief overwhelmed me so that I had to put my story away in order to continue to fulfill the responsibilities my life required of me, for I had not yet felt the full measure of my grief. I feel deep within myself that now is the time. It may not be for the benefit of others, though I hope there are those who will be comforted by my words, but it is for my own healing that this story must be told. I cannot promise answers to the questions such a tragedy awakens. Yet, I feel strongly that I need to produce something in regard to my father's death. In some small way, it is as though the writing of this book will ensure that his death was not in vain. He would have gladly laid down his life for another. If through the words held within this book I can help one person, then I will feel that his loss has not been without a purpose. My hope is that in sharing my journey, some comfort, remedy, or resolution may come to the reader.

I do not claim to have all the answers or that I have grown so wise as to instruct others. In no way am I implying this is the way everyone should feel; that this is what everyone should believe. I only know what I have experienced and the conclusions, if any, I have reached. Read on and know only that this is what has come to me.

# SONNET XXX

When to the sessions of sweet silent thought
I summon up remembrance of things past,
I sigh the lack of many a thing I sought,
And with old woes new wail my dear time's waste;
Then can I drown an eye, unused to flow,
For precious friends hid in death's dateless night,
And weep afresh love's long-since-cancelled woe,
And moan th' expense of many a vanished sight;
Then can I grieve at grievances foregone,
And heavily from woe to woe tell o'er
The sad account of fore-bemoanèd moan,
Which I new pay as if not paid before.
But if the while I think on thee, dear friend,
All losses are restored and sorrows end.
~William Shakespeare[1]

# Episode 1

# FOREVER CHANGED

*It seemed a thousand years ago*
*and on the other side of the world.*
*~ J. R. R. Tolkien[1]*

How do I begin? How do I tell the tale of all that has happened? Ten years it has been, as I sit here trying to put down the thoughts and feelings that have occurred since that day. It seems insurmountable to place into words all that has transpired, yet I feel a need to try. So how do I begin?

It is a tale wrought with anguish and woe, and yet, as I look back, as I walked in the dark path of suffering, I see more clearly that it is also a tale that has always been a Pharos that shone upon the way, though I could not see it at the beginning. But it was there, always there summoning me, as a beacon of light piercing the darkness, calling out to me from around the bend. All I needed to do was take a few more steps, and then I would have seen it. That is how it often is when trials come. We are blinded by our sorrow and fear to all that is available to help us. And so it happened.

God let me down. It was a beautiful morning. The sun shone brightly. A faint breeze brushed through leaves painted with gold

1

and red, whispering of autumn. The blush of day was still and silent, as though inhaling a breath and holding onto it, waiting to exhale. Suddenly, the sound of engines roaring broke through the air, growing ever louder. In an instant, no life would be the same; my life would never be the same.

The events of September 11, 2001, mark a change in my life. On that day, my precious father, Stanley R. Hall, was ripped from this world as American Airlines Flight 77 plummeted into the Pentagon in Washington, DC. Numb and dazed, we walked those first months. FBI agents, memorial services, honors given, all a haze of lost senses.

How did we become entangled in this? How did my family get caught up in this conflict? I cannot answer these questions. All I know is that I am forever changed, marked by the wound of that day. I look back at pictures taken before September 11 and think, *that was before, when we were innocent, before everything changed.* I see myself as a different person than the woman in those photographs. Life is much more serious now. A shadow of mourning hovers over me each day. Living with grief is hard. The moment I realized my father was aboard the plane was like being slapped in the face for no reason. My breath escaped me. My chest constricted, crushing me with the weight of loss. For days, I was unable to swallow, except to swallow the grief.

That morning, I was ignorant of what was happening outside the walls of my bustling household. I was busy preparing for the day. Besides homeschooling my three children, I had just taken on the responsibility of running the children's program at our church. I had planned to spend that beautiful September morning working at church, preparing the children's church room. I was in the process of packing the car to make ready for the week's activities, taking schoolwork for the kids, when the phone rang.

*The phone rang.* If only I had not picked it up, I could have stayed the sorrow that was to follow. But I did pick it up; ignorant of what lay before me with the words that would soon follow my cheerful hello.

"Where's Daddy?" my brother asked, urgency in his voice.

Confusion swept over me. My brother was in Rochester, New York. Why was he calling me? My father lived in Virginia. I was in Texas. How should I know where he was at that moment?

"Turn on the TV. Don't you know the world's coming to an end?" he cried.

He told me he had tried to call our mother, but all the lines were down in Virginia. He couldn't get through to her.

I reached for the remote and turned on the TV. Horror filled my eyes as the news broadcast the planes flying into the World Trade Center. Then, as the nation let out a collective gasp, the towers collapsed. A cloud of dust and debris filled the city. *All those people.* Tears streamed from my eyes, yet I had no idea that our family would be pulled so personally into this tragedy. Then word came that the Pentagon had been struck. My father often worked in the Pentagon. My heart paused.

Through his company's headquarters in Virginia, my husband was able to get through to my mother. She told us that my father was safe, for his plane to California had left earlier that morning. That was when fear began to take me. While I calculated events as the newscast pronounced them, I began to realize that the timing of the plane's takeoff might mean that he was not safe. I held my breath.

Just as my mother was looking up my father's flight itinerary, the newscast stated that Flight 77 had been the plane that crashed into the Pentagon. My husband repeated my mother's words as I entered his office to tell him which flight it had been. I heard him say those words, words etched in my memory. "Flight 77." I took in a breath. I wanted to scream. No. It couldn't be. God would not let this happen to my father, he was always okay. He was the one who always took care of us. Nothing could happen to him. He would surely call and say, "Guess what happened to me on the way to the airport?"

My husband looked sorrowfully into my eyes and with a broken voice said, "I'm so sorry." Horror struck, I returned his gaze. My mother hung on the phone. He must have told her that it was my father's flight that crashed into the Pentagon, but I do not recall what followed. I stood aghast, unbelieving. Then I thought of my mother listening on the other end of the phone. What do I do?

I ran from the room. I did not want my mother to hear me sobbing. My first thought was that life was over. In an instant, the culmination of all my hopes and dreams came crashing down. There was no need to go on. Nothing would be the same. I did not care what happened to me. Death could take me. That would be all right. My heart was hollow, echoing of loss, each breath a struggle, each moment something to endure. What was the point of going on? All was lost. It was over.

Overcome, I collapsed on the floor. My two oldest children, then ten and six, ran over and wrapped their precious little arms around me, the remnant of him. Confused, they held their sobbing mother as I cried, "No, no, no" over and over again.

As I knelt there on the floor, cradling my body within my arms, I told myself, *pull it together. You are carrying on for no reason. Daddy is going to call. We don't even know for sure if he was aboard the plane. Stop crying and stand up. You are getting ahead of yourself.* But what if it were true? What if he was dead? It was beyond my comprehension. After a time, I got up. I had to get control of myself. My little ones needed me.

I went to my husband and asked, "What do I do?"

He looked at me and said, "Pack your suitcase."

Puzzled, I returned his gaze for a moment and then asked, "What do I put in a suitcase?"

I have spent my life traveling, packing many suitcases, but in that moment, I had forgotten. Numb, I turned and went upstairs. Previously, I had purchased a black dress. As of then, I had not had an occasion to wear it. I laid the dress upon the bed next to my suitcase. I refused to pack it. Black dresses were what you wore to funerals. The dress wouldn't be needed; I knew my father would call. He just couldn't get through. The phone lines were down. That was all. But the call never came.

My husband was finally able to contact the airlines. The representative confirmed that my father had checked in, but could not establish that he had actually boarded the plane. I knew he had. He would not have checked in and not boarded. Finally, I carefully placed my new black dress inside the suitcase and closed the lid. That was that. This is what it is.

All I could think was *get to Mother.* She was alone. We were in Texas; she was in Virginia. Never before had I felt so far away. My uncle lived in Maryland, my sister also; only an hour's drive away from my mother's house, but Washington, DC was shut down. The Beltway was closed. There was no easy way for anyone to get from Maryland to Virginia. She was all alone. All planes were grounded. There was nothing else to do but drive the long hours to Virginia.

I called my close friend to tell her what had happened and to let her know we were leaving town. Stunned, she asked if she could come over to be with me. I told her no. I was afraid that if she came to comfort me I would fall apart. I had to be strong. I had much to do, and I could not afford to break down. There would be time enough to grieve, but at that moment, I had to get to Virginia.

Hours slipped by. By late afternoon, it was reported that Al-Qaeda, a terrorist group of radical Muslims, claimed responsibility for the attacks. With this added knowledge, we began to prepare for the trip. We needed to get the car in good order. Anesthetized by shock, I dropped my husband off to run an errand, and then I took the car to get the oil changed. As the kids and I waited in the lobby, the news was on the TV, showing us over and over again the unfolding of terror. There was the Pentagon, its walls collapsed and burning. How could my father be in the midst of those flames? I looked away. The shop had a LEGO table set up, so I watched the kids build towers with the blocks as I held my eleven month old in my lap.

"Look, Mommy," they called, "our planes are crashing into the buildings."

A shock wave ran down my body. But I let them play, aware they were trying to make sense of the senseless, trying to come to terms with what their innocent eyes were forced to witness. Their lives

> So much death…
> what can men do
> against such
> reckless hate?
> – *The Two Towers*[2]

would never be the same. They would have to live in this world, now so touched by hate.

In the stillness that followed September 11, the silent emptiness filled us with the stunned awe of disbelief. How could anyone do such a thing, such a terrible thing? How can we live in a world so full of hate?

So we drove, twenty-three hours stopping only for food and fuel. Twenty-three hours with three children, one of them a baby, cramped for what seemed like endless hours in the backseat. There was not a sound of complaint, not a whimper of discomfort as the hours stretched on through the night and into the opening of the next day. We kept the radio off, shutting our minds from the events that had occurred. The car was silent; the skies were dark, the hours rolled by. I sat stunned in my seat.

My aunt and uncle from Maryland finally made it through DC and stayed with my mother for a few hours until my brother from New York arrived. We finally reached my mother's house on the afternoon of the twelfth. We came through the door tired and grieved. We fell into waiting arms, clung to one another, and sobbed.

> O shut the door,
> and when thou hast done so,
> Come weep with me—past hope, past care,
> past help!
> - Shakespeare[3]

How strange to walk this earth after death had come. I had experienced death before. Working as an oncology nurse, I had often held the hand of cancer patients as they slipped from this world into the next. It always struck me how surreal are the moments after death. How can the world and its people carry on as though nothing had happened? It is like looking through a lens, watching the events of life unfolding, yet without being part of it. In that moment, life stands still for the grieved, yet the rest of the world continues its pace through time uninterrupted. I wanted to shout, "What are you doing? Don't you know someone has died? How can you go on as though nothing has changed?"

Well-meaning people would tell me, "Don't worry, everything will be okay." They would hug me or pat my back as though they could wipe away the sorrow. But how could everything be okay? You cannot fix everything. You cannot undo death. How will this ever be okay?

How do you go back?

> How do you pick up the threads of an old life? How do you go on, when in your heart you begin to understand there 'is' no going back? There are some things time cannot mend. Some hurts that go too deep... that have taken hold.
>
> *– Return of the King*[4]

# Episode 2

# AWAKENED

*The grief was still too near,*
*a matter for tears and not yet for song.*
*~J. R. R. Tolkien*[1]

You just sit and try to understand. But some things cannot be understood. Some paths are just too dark to see the other side, and once you have turned down the path there's no going back. It's dark and no one can take the journey for you. There is nothing but forward, though you do it with trembling and uncertainty. This journey is not of my choosing, but it is mine nonetheless.

When we arrived at my mother's house on September 12, 2001, it soon became evident that we were all in shock. My brother, a world traveler, should have given no thought to preparing for a trip. Yet, thinking of his need for comfort, he only packed socks and boxes of tea in his luggage. I, on the other hand, did not pack one single pair of socks. My daughter, who originally tried to bring every article of clothing she owned, ended up removing all but a few shirts. For two weeks I wore my brother's socks, my daughter wore his shirts, and he, having not yet removed all his belongings from the house since leaving home, had to wear his old clothes. We had a brief moment of levity over this situation, a needed break from the serious grief and tension that hung over us.

The next morning, my mother came downstairs, moving quickly, as though urgency propelled her, her eyes wide, her lips tightly set. Her behavior was wild and desperate. I was unnerved. I suppose all of us appeared disheveled and in shock. We kept the TV off. For several weeks, we did not watch the news. None of us could bear to witness the events replayed over and over again.

At first, we were not allowed to move anything in the house. "Don't move that," my mother would cry. "That is where Daddy left it. Leave it there." We didn't want to change anything. I found it hard to clean the house for it felt as though I was wiping away the last remnants of my father's presence. Even with all the people who had congregated within the house, it felt empty. How profound is the awareness of one missing soul. I kept listening for the garage door to open and hear my father's footsteps on the hardwood floor.

Men in black suits began to appear on the doorstep. Grim looks pressed on their faces as they attended to their appointed task, the business of death. The FBI was responsible for investigating the terrorist attacks; therefore, each family of a victim was visited and questioned. These young men, never having dealt with such an event before, though professional, appeared as stunned as we were. Yet, the questions came and we answered, unfolding the story of our lives before them. Some of the questions were quite personal in nature; they were trying to learn anything that might

> **The Bustle in a House**
> The bustle in a house
> The morning after death
> Is solemnest of industries
> Enacted upon earth.
>
> The sweeping up
> the heart,
> And putting love away
> We shall not want to
> use again
> Until eternity.
> –Emily Dickinson[2]

help them identify my father's remains. Nothing would be left unknown.

My mother kept saying, "Why do you need to know all this. He's all burned up; there's nothing left. He's all burned up."

Indeed, his body was broken and burned. My brother gave blood for DNA sampling, in case my father's body was recovered. It was then that the realization of what had happened hit home. This was no ordinary death. This was, in fact, a murder investigation. Is this how all families of murder victims feel? My heart went out to them. My chest was ripped open, my heart torn out, twisted, and then shoved back in again.

But, we were not alone. I knew somewhere in America, three thousand families were going through what we were experiencing now. They were hurting and suffering just as we were. So much pain. Something moves you through the hours, those empty hours of despair. Robotically, I took each step as though controlled by the great manipulator who pulls the strings from above, yet hidden from view, causing the marionette to move as directed. So the business of grieving waited as we moved through the questions and procedures.

My father's car remained parked at the airport, waiting for him to retrieve it. But he would never come. His umbrella rested, propped up against the passenger seat, just as he had left it. His hand would never touch the umbrella again. My husband and brother traveled to the airport and were questioned by the FBI before they could claim the car. No one knew who the enemy was, so all were to be examined. My husband, sparing my brother the pain of sitting in his father's car, drove the vehicle home. They returned the car to its usual spot as though nothing had happened. Each time I walked past the car, I looked at it knowing my father would never back it out of the garage again. My heart burned within me.

Life is swift. How soon we find ourselves cut off. "Oh God, do not forget me in the anguish of my soul! My hope is spent, and my eyes will no more see good for the shadow of grief has overcome me and hope has vanished from my sight."

How like Job I feel (who lost everything; his possessions, his health, and even his children to death) as I "speak in the anguish of my spirit" and "complain in the bitterness of my soul" for "he who goes down to the grave does not come up." (Job 7:6-11) My father shall never come home again. I will nevermore see his face in this world. Therefore, I will not hold back, I will speak what is in my heart.

Flags at half-mast lined the roadway as we traveled to my sister's house in Maryland a few days later. Jeeps with antiaircraft missiles flanked the highway en route to the Pentagon as we made our way to the Beltway that circumscribes Washington, DC. It was surreal, as if we were watching the news about some distant war-torn country. It felt as though we were in a battle zone, then again, I suppose we were. My heart pounded, a feeling I have come to expect,

Stan was known as the "Father of EW" by most people involved in electronic warfare. Having worked at Litton, Hughes, Raytheon, and other companies, Stan contributed to just about every existing American EW system in use today. Stan conceived of the ALR-67(V)3 Countermeasures Receiving System.... Stan typified the finest... a true gentleman; quiet, unassuming, absolutely competent; a gifted engineer, and a man of great personal integrity and honor.

> – Jack Saunders
> Director Integrated Systems
> Raytheon EW Systems

as we approached the Pentagon, its wound still smoldering, blackened, and scarred. The highway passed just within view of the devastation. There were those who lost loved ones at the Pentagon who flocked to the site. They seemed to have felt drawn to the place where their family member died. A makeshift memorial had sprung up displaying signs and pictures and flowers. People crowded around the area, longing for a glimpse, a place to feel close to the lost. I couldn't bear it. I turned away. I could not look

COMMANDER
NAVAL AIR SYSTEMS COMMAND
PATUXENT RIVER, MARYLAND  20670-1161

19 September 2001

Dear Mrs. Hall,

On behalf of the men and women of Naval Air Systems Command, I would like to extend my sincerest and deepest sympathy to you and all members of your family on the tragic loss of your husband, Stanley. He devoted his life in dedicated and patriotic service to a nation he loved. You can be justifiably proud of Stanley's many accomplishments. Your husband was most respected and all of Naval Aviation will miss him. We share in your great loss.

Again, our hearts, thoughts, and prayers are with you in these very trying times.

Sincerely,

J. W. DYER
Vice Admiral, U. S. Navy

upon the site. My breath caught in my chest. My lungs felt like they could burst. Then we passed by, my heart began to settle and my breathing leveled. But the emptiness remained.

Empty. We had no body, no casket. Nothing. It soon became clear how important it was to have remains to bury. The mind cannot comprehend the loss, the death, without some tangible evidence. It was as though my father walked out the door and vanished. We were waiting, waiting for closure, but none would come. I told my mother that we had to plan a memorial service. People had traveled to be with us and were waiting. They all needed closure. We could not wait for my father's remains, for they may never be found. So on September 20, 2001, we held a service. The church ascended in the distance as we made our way down the tree lined roadway. Family and friends gathered to celebrate the life that was led. My father. I had no idea how great a man he had really been.

Integrity, honor, unassuming… a common thread in all the condolence letters we received.

In Nancy Fleischer's letter, she mentions my father's quiet calm. I remember that *quiet calm*, the way he made everyone feel safe. Once when I was a young girl playing softball, I started having trouble breathing. Panic set in as the asthma took hold. Then I felt the hands of my father around my ribs as he calmly held me. He pushed the air out of my lungs so I could take the next breath. He didn't say anything, but the fear lost its hold on me. I calmed as I sensed his presence. My air came easier as I felt safe in his embrace.

And so here we were to say our final farewell to this man I called Father. Rejoicing and sorrow mingled; love and grief united as one, as the death march began down the aisle. A silver-framed image was placed before us, a shadow of him gone away. How

To:     stanleyhallcondolences@raytheon.com
cc:

Subject: Condolences


A letter to the family of Stan Hall

I knew Stan, by reputation, long before I had the pleasure of his
friendship. He was so well respected in the professional circles of
Electronic Warfare, it would be impossible to be in this field without
having heard his name- a respect that was well deserved. I finally met him
in the early 90's. We were engineering colleagues. Knowing him and having
his advice, support and technical help throughout these past years has
enriched my life in immeasurable ways and after the events of September 11,
will be a most cherished memory.

Stan was an inspiration - beyond a mentor. His laughter, his smile, his
gentleness, his perseverance, his perspective, his genius, his quiet calm,
his encouragement, his knowledge, his experience, his work, his integrity?
I will miss him. We will miss him.

His contribution to the defense of our country has been significant and
creates an irony beyond comprehension in this attack against us. Many of
our leaders, both military and industrial, have called upon Stan for advice
regarding electronic technologies and the applications for electronic
warfare. His work has directly enhanced the survivability of military
aircraft and the servicemen who fly them. His ultimate legacy will be in
saving the life of one who will defend us against these terrorists that
threaten our way of life.

It was a pleasure and a privilege to have known him.

My heart goes out to you and your family. I will be praying for His
continued grace and support for all of you.


Sincerely,

Nancy Fleischer

can someone be here one minute, and then gone the next, vacant from this world? It all seemed so unreal.

After two weeks of dealing with the aftermath of September 11, our family returned home. I was to resume the threads of a normal life. But how could life ever be normal again? Outwardly, I performed all that was expected. Inwardly, I felt as though I was moving through a thick fog, dazed and confused. Within days of arriving home, we celebrated our youngest son's birthday. I sat there looking on, knowing that I needed to cherish the moment, this first birthday of my last child, but really, I wasn't even there.

I felt nothing. I was numb. My son's entire life has been his mother trying to come to terms with 9/11. Yet somehow, I walked through the days and months that followed. The school year continued, more birthdays came; then the holidays approached, and the weariness set in.

Life is hard. Just the breath we take in can become a burden. There were days when all I could do was focus on the next moment, for to look beyond that next moment was overwhelming. I would go through the day saying, "All I am going to do is unload the dishwasher. That is all I have to do. I will think of nothing but unloading the dishwasher." Then I would swallow the tears and unload the dishwasher.

> You are worn with sorrow and much toil.
> ~J. R. R. Tolkien[3]

Then I would say, "Now I am going to load the dishwasher. I will think of nothing but loading the dishwasher...." Moment to moment was all I could handle. I wanted to throw the covers over my head and stay in bed forever. But I had a baby who needed me, so I got up and faced each new day, each day where no dawn could reach me.

The terror of it all surrounds me. Though I would shake it off, it pursues me, violently storming against me. How can I outrun the wind? The more I leave off, the more it seeks me out. My soul is poured out in my distress. I am dissolved in a flood of tears, my vessel full of holes so that nothing is contained. "The days of affliction take hold of me." (Job 30:15-16)

How can God understand my hurt? "Does He have eyes of flesh? Or does He see as man sees?" (Job 10:4) Even worse, if He grasps how I feel, how could He let this happen knowing full well how this would affect me? If God is Love, how can He allow Hate to strike His own?

# Episode 3

# TEARS

*I will not say: do not weep;*
*for not all tears are an evil.*

*~J. R. R. Tolkien*[1]

And the tears come. Will they ever stop? At times, they take hold of you, grasping every fiber of your body as a fever produces rigors. Why do we cry? It changes nothing. Weeping cannot bring anyone back. Those tears, they are traitors, coming upon me unawares no matter where I am or what I am doing. A simple trip to the grocery store can release a fountain of tears. A flood of emotion overcomes me as I reach for a jar of boysenberry jam. "Daddy always liked that jelly. He'll never eat it again." And the tears come.

Even now, when I tell someone for the first time what happened to my father, my heart pounds, my hands shake, and my breath shortens. I can be moving innocently through my day, and then a thought crosses my mind and the tears come. I never know when the sorrow will overtake me. People must look at me and wonder what is wrong. I can be listening to a sermon in church or watching a movie in the theater, and it hits me, that treasonous fountain of liquid grief.

The weeks following 9/11 were the worst, especially my fight-or-flight reactions. To this day, low-flying airplanes make me shudder. My heart races and my chest constricts at the sound of the engines overhead. At first, I had trouble driving; every time a car drew near, my startle reflex took over. I would gasp and overreact. I even scraped the car across the side of our brick house. As I was trying to make the turn around our garage, which is in the rear of our house, I took the turn too sharply. With a horrendous grating sound, the car scraped across the brick leaving a mar across the crisp black paint. My husband came running out of

> When words fail, tears flow. Tears have a language all their own, a tongue that needs no interpreter. In some mysterious way, our complex inner-communication system knows when to admit its verbal limitations... and the tears come.... Tears are not self-conscious. They can spring upon us when we are speaking in public, or standing beside others who look to us for strength. Most often they appear when our soul is overwhelmed with feelings that words cannot describe.
>
> – Charles Swindoll[2]

the house to find me crying in the front seat. He was very patient and loving as I sobbed, "I am a menace to society, a danger on the road. You need to take my license away!"

He calmly told me to drive away and continue my day as planned. He would call the insurance company and take care of everything. In his wisdom, he knew that if I did not drive away right then, I would never drive again. So, very cautiously, I drove the kids to the park. Of course, to my embarrassment, as soon as we got to the park, the kids ran over to our friends and told them what I had done. So I cried.

Shortly after 9/11, I looked into the mirror and saw my father's eyes looking back at me. Funny, how I never noticed before that I had his eyes. I could hardly look at myself without

> There's a grief that can't
> be spoken,
> There's a pain goes on
> and on.
> Empty chairs at empty tables
> now my friends are dead
> and gone.
> ~ Les Miserables [3]

acutely experiencing the loss. The hollow feeling left behind, rests heavily on my heart. Tight chest and trembling hands is all that's left now that he is gone. "Daddy, you are always on my mind."

I felt young before September 11. That event aged me more than years ever could. I have trouble with all things superficial. I am very serious, dark at times. I feel an urgency to get things done, convinced that I will die young. What if I die before I can accomplish everything I feel so strongly I need to do?

I began to get sick just three weeks after September 11. My immune system seems to have been affected; I get ill much easier now. I have aches and pains that come and go. I feel like my body is attacking itself. Some nights, sleep eludes me. And there is depression, always lurking in the background. At times, it reaches out and takes hold of me. "The mind is its own place, and in itself can make a heaven of hell, a hell of heaven…" (Milton, lines 254-255).[4]

One month after September 11, I drove the kids by myself to Dallas to attend the State Fair of Texas. As we entered the congestion of the city, my oldest son began complaining of a stomachache. At the age of six, he was keenly aware of all that had happened. Anxiety plagued his little life. Once we arrived at the fair, his symptoms subsided, and we had a lovely time together looking at exhibits, going on rides, and touring museums. I was proud of my accomplishment, driving three small children all the way to Dallas and back. My own anxiety had taken a backseat to my resolve to provide a distraction for my children.

Since the loss of his grandfather, my oldest son began having regressive behaviors, stomachaches, and headaches. After determining that there was no physical reason for his difficulties, I took him to a grief counselor. He spoke with both of us and determined that my son was responding to my grief. As I would heal, so would my son. With that information, I grew determined to find a way to overcome my sorrow. I tried to protect him from what I was experiencing. I wanted my son to heal, even if I was unable. He did improve. I seemed to be better also, so I stopped going for counseling, feeling I was able to move forward on my own.

However, as time wore on, I began to fall back into the throes of grief, and I decided to return to the grief counselor. I soon learned, however, that the counselor had died of a heart attack. He was only forty-eight. I could not believe this was happening. Were all the good Christian men being taken from my life? Just when the world needed men like my father and my counselor, they were taken away. It made no sense to me.

The counselors provided by the Pentagon informed us that the events of 9/11 could even traumatize infants. For years, whenever I would leave the house without the children, my youngest son, who had been an infant in 2001, would become frantic. Many times, I would get a call on my cell phone, asking me to come back. He feared that he would never see his mother again. I would turn the car around and return home. My littlest son would be waiting for me. I would take him in my arms, kiss him, and tell him that I loved him. Then he would be okay and I would run my errand.

I found it difficult to sit in church listening to the uplifting praise choruses. Everyone was so happy. I didn't feel like praising

God or singing happy songs. I needed something more, something deeper that spoke to the hole in my soul.

Often as I drove down the road that fall of 2001, I noticed the changing leaves waving gently against the clear blue sky. My father would never see autumn, the leaves in their glory, changing colors. He would never see his grandchildren grow and never know what they would one day become. My father would never meet his namesake, my brother's son, named for the grandfather he will never know. I wanted my father to walk through the door. If only he would just walk through that door and say it was all a bad dream.

I used to see someone driving down the road in his car, with white hair similar to my father's, and I would take a second look. I knew it wasn't he, but still, I had to look again to make sure. When I confirmed it was someone else, my shoulders sank and I sighed. I would see a man older than my father and think to myself, *my father never had the opportunity to grow old. He was never able to retire and live out his golden years to enjoy the benefits of his labor.*

Sometime after September 11, I believe it was the spring of 2002, we were visiting my mother. When it was time to catch our flight home, my oldest son developed a migraine and began vomiting. I told my husband there was no way our son could fly in his condition. My husband suggested that he take the other two children home and leave me at my mother's house with my son until the next day. I flipped out. I could not bear to separate our family.

I shouted, "If we go down, we go down together! I am not going through this again!"

My poor husband had to change all five of our tickets and pay the penalty fee for each one, because I could not handle flying on separate airplanes.

I am damaged. I need to dig down inside myself and use the wound as strength not as a weakness. I need to caress it, grasp it, let it make me strong. Yet, at times, the weight of it is more than I can bear. So I cry as Job did, and "speak in the bitterness of my soul." (Job 10:1)

I cannot fully explain what happens to someone when grief strikes. The subconscious mind is always aware of the loss. It invades all that one tries to do. Can I ever hope again? Each year since September 2001, as the date draws near, I begin to grow restless and agitated. My temper flares, fatigue sets in, and I become depressed. All this begins without my conscious awareness that the anniversary of 9/11 is approaching. How can the body know even while the mind is not cognizant? I sense the change in my demeanor, so I stop and think. As I realize the advancing anniversary, I say, "Oh, yes, I know what is happening."

The trauma of September 11 was most profound the first three months following the event. Dreams came, or should I say nightmares. I would dream that I was on Flight 77, witnessing firsthand what happened to the people as the plane crashed. Seeing my father die over and over again, hoping it was quick so he did not suffer. Then I would find myself at the World Trade Center trying in desperation to convince the firefighters not to enter the buildings, but to no avail, they could not see or hear me. I felt helpless to prevent what I knew would come. Even now, I often wake from sleep to feel my face grimacing, my hands clenching, and my shoulders tight.

As Christmas of 2001 approached, the effects enacted upon me by the trauma of 9/11 reached a pinnacle as it flooded into all areas of my life. We had been informed during the week of Thanksgiving 2001 that my father's remains had been identified. My mother and brother spent the holiday arranging for my father's internment. It was decided to have the burial just prior to Christmas in order to accommodate work and travel schedules for various family members.

Even though we had to leave before Christmas to bury my father, my husband, and I decided to decorate the house and celebrate the holidays with the children at home before we had to face what lay ahead. We wanted to give them a sense of normalcy. For me Christmas would never be the same. In trying to decorate the tree, I had to focus intently so as not to drop the ornaments, for my hands shook all the time. Carefully, I climbed the ladder and gently, deliberately, I placed each ornament upon a limb. Every ornament represented a memory. Each memory brought forth tears and sorrow with which I had to deal. It was like having my fingernails ripped out one by one, and then going back for more. Christmas had always felt magical to me. I loved everything about it. I loved the food and family, the decorations and gift giving, everything. Now I felt nothing. I was numb. Empty. Eventually, I began dropping the ornaments. I tried to make my fingers work, but they refused. Fumbling with incoordination, my fingers felt as though they belonged to someone else. It was enough. The tree would do partially decorated.

As it was, I could not focus long enough to keep track of bills or shopping. My loving husband had to take on the burden. I was just trying to get through each day. I ventured to the mall. That was difficult. My husband had taken care of all the Christmas shopping, except his own present. So I tried. The mall was bright and happy. Christmas music was playing; people were bustling through the stores merry with the promise of the season. My grief caught in my throat, but I swallowed it. I thought I would buy my husband a new jacket for work. I held two up to examine them closer, and then I began to panic. "What jackets did he already have? Does he have this one? What if he doesn't like it? What color should I get?"

Decisions. I could not make up my mind. Here my husband had carried us all through the months since September 11, and I couldn't even buy him a Christmas present. I left the store. I couldn't do it. He would have to take care of that also. I felt defeated. The simple tasks of life had become overwhelming.

American Airlines flew us first class to Washington, DC to attend my father's burial. As I sat in the seat, I knew my father had been in first class on September 11. Where had he sat? What had he been thinking as the hijackers took over the plane? Had he been frightened? Had he thought about his family? Did he know he was going to die that day? My mind swam with images and thoughts. I had never really feared flying. I didn't fear it then, but I could not help thinking about the last moments of my father's life in an airplane. It was hard not to fall apart in front of everyone. I did not want my children to fear flying or to see me lose it, so I choked down the tears.

March 2002 rolled around, and the White House invited the victims' families to the Rose Garden to honor the six-month anniversary. We met at Arlington National Cemetery. As we stood among the graves of fallen heroes, waiting to board the buses that would transport us to the White House, I looked beyond the thousands of headstones to the wounded who stood with me. Wide-eyed and tearful, they stood displaying the emotional and physical scars of 9/11. Some, like us, were family members of a lost loved one. A few were victims that had survived the brutal attack, their bodies maimed and scarred. All present had a faraway look in their eyes, of disbelief and shock, the same look I had. Would we, could we, ever come to terms with the outcome of September 11?

Strict security clearance was needed to enter beyond the gates of the Rose Garden. My uncle and I escorted my mother to this event. We made it through the first security checkpoint without difficulty. As we attempted to enter the second security point, we realized my uncle's and my names were not on the list. My mother had entered through the gates. She looked back at us with fear in her eyes, as the two of us were not permitted to enter. I gazed at her feeling her distress. In her eyes, I saw the helpless panic we were all experiencing. This entire tragedy had ripped the very foundation out from under us, and we were sinking. How vulnerable my mother looked standing there alone as emotion began to overwhelm her.

Our Master Sargent spoke to the FBI on our behalf, cleared up the miscommunication, and allowed my uncle and me to rejoin my mother. Once inside, we took our places among the grieving family members. As I sat listening to the president address the crowd, I could not help but notice soldiers armed with sniper rifles lining the roof. The reality of the world we lived in settled upon me as I looked at these dark images of men crouching down with gun barrels aimed across the crowd. Rising, we stood in solemn respect as the names of each lost at the Pentagon were remembered.

It was the first time I had left my baby for so long. I found it difficult to leave him and venture alone to Virginia to be with my mother. This event marked one of many that would take me away from home to honor my father's memory.

In May 2002, my brother graduated from Eastman University with his doctorate. After all the years of study, all the time that my father had supported my brother while he worked hard for his education, my father would not be there to see him graduate. My father should have been there. My brother turned to look at my mother and I as his row stood to receive their doctoral certificates. In his expression, I saw the face of my father. My father's absence was painfully evident.

In 2002, the one-year anniversary of 9/11, our family went to the Pentagon for the opening of a memorial dedicated to the 184 victims who died in the building and on Flight 77. Our chairs were set on the lawn on the very spot where the plane had crashed into the Pentagon. Flying proudly above the crowd, raised high upon a crane, flew an American flag. Under the flag was a sign that boldly stated Tom Beamer's immortal words, "Let's Roll!"

The Pentagon before us was restored, the scars of the impact removed, and new blocks stood defiant. Yet, we sat with our wounds exposed. We had not rebuilt our lives. The hole in our hearts remained. At the site is a memorial chapel with a beautifully handmade stained glass created in memory of those who perished. Also within the area of the crash site is a wall, the America's Heroes Memorial. The monument consists of a large black acrylic wall that houses the engraved names of each person who had died that day. Strips of paper were available so we could make a rubbing of our loved one's name. I picked up the paper and walked to where my father's name was inscribed. Drawing the pencil across the paper, I saw his name begin to rise onto the page. While I watched his name appear across the white surface, I was overcome. How was I even there making that rubbing? Seeing my father's name materialize upon the slip of paper seemed to solidify the fact that my father was dead.

As I rose from where I kneeled, tears poured from my eyes. My cry was audible. Several counselors descended upon me as I fell apart. My husband grabbed me, enveloping me in his embrace. I melted into his arms and sobbed.

The FBI presented us with a very large binder filled with pictures of the personal effects found at the crash site. Our assignment was to look upon each image to determine if any were the belongings of our loved one. As we sat turning the pages, we gazed upon the wreckage of 184 ruined lives. The photos in this book represented all that remained of so many people. Trinkets and articles of little value, scorched and scarred, left behind by the dead. Ironically, it was my father's frequent flyer card that was recovered, his name still visible upon the damaged card. The edges burned. A singed hole in the corner marked the trauma inflicted.

As we struggled with our grief, the United States attorney general was preparing to prosecute Zacarias Moussaoui for his involvement in the September 11 attacks. As a member of a victim's family, I continually received information from the attorney general's office in relation to the proceedings. Due to the ongoing investigation, the public was not made privy to information regarding the events as they took place within the hijacked planes. In order to assist the victims' families in their desire for more information, family members were invited to attend a meeting at FBI headquarters in Washington DC where full disclosure would be made. After much consideration, several members of my family and I chose to attend the meeting.

Nervously, we walked down the sidewalk beside the J. Edgar

Hoover building. A multitude of flags rose from the side of the building as though saluting all who walked below. Upon entering, we were instructed to leave behind all cell phones and cameras. Visitor passes were issued and we signed a confidentiality agreement before entering the conference room.

Counselors were stationed outside the meeting room, provided for our use if needed. An FBI agent stood before us and described in detail the events as they unfolded, and then we heard the recordings of all phone calls and radio contacts made. As I sat there listening to the last words spoken by people aboard the planes, just moments before their deaths, I felt as though I was witnessing firsthand the terror of that day. The desire to help them was overwhelming. I cried within myself, *somebody do something! Help them!* But I knew there was nothing to be done. The voices had been silenced long ago. All that was left to do was weep.

Years later, at the September 11, 2008 dedication of the Pentagon Memorial Benches, a bell tolled as each of the 184 names was spoken. Each strike echoed through my soul, each knell representing a life lost. I felt grief for every one of them. So many people senselessly taken from those who loved them. And for what? Was anything gained? My youngest son was only a baby when the horror of September 11 occurred. As I sat there weeping, he kept asking, "Why is Mommy crying?" I could not answer him, for the tears took my voice.

All I know is that all must suffer loss and grief in this world. No one has ever *not* walked this path. It is a universal truth that all have suffered and for each who has, his or her grief is the greatest. Yet, when one who is loved is taken, we cannot help but look back at what has been lost. It is a glimmer of passing light, a

Part of every misery is, so to speak, the misery's shadow or reflection: the fact that you don't merely suffer but have to keep on thinking about the fact that you suffer. I not only live each endless day in grief, but live each day thinking about living each day in grief. Do these notes merely aggravate that side of it? Merely confirm the monotonous, treadmill march of the mind round one subject?... By writing it all down... I believe I get a little outside it.

~ C. S. Lewis[5]

deep breath in the torrents of life that helps us to linger, if only for a moment, on thoughts of those who mold us. For it is the love we share with others that makes us who we are. Time and torrents shape us, carve the image of the trials etched upon our lives, yet it is the love offered by others that preserves us against the erosion of life. So we pause and wonder. Memories haunt our thoughts, they sneak up and jar us unawares, and then the heartache grabs us and grief spills out as we melt into a puddle of emotion.

Memories, those distant thoughts that bind us to our past, cause so much pain... and comfort. I miss the sound of my father's footsteps upon the wood floor as he came home each night. I miss hearing the soft creak of the stairs late at night when all others had gone to bed. His sneezing in the morning, the look upon his face as he silently sat and watched as the family gathered. His "How about that" so often said, his meaning clear "I love you." I miss his resolve to lead a life of integrity, and honor, and steadfastness, his quiet and resolute spirit to follow God wherever He led, to whatever end.

*The dying groan in the city, And the souls of the wounded cry out; Yet God does not charge them with wrong.*
-Job 24:12

"What strength do I have, that I should hope?" (Job 6:11a) My mind is like a house filled with archways. I have no doors that I can shut against the grief. My sorrow flows freely into all aspects of my life. I can never escape it. "I am not at ease, nor am I quiet; I have no rest, for trouble comes." (Job 3:26)

And so the tears come as the loss overwhelms, like a wave that crashes into me and tosses me, threatening to drag me out to sea. Each new memory casts me back into the grief and loss. The emptiness consumes me, a fire that cannot be extinguished.

# Episode 4

# SILENCE

*Vindicate me, O God,*
*And plead my cause against an ungodly nation;*
*Oh, deliver me from the deceitful and unjust man!*
*For You are the God of my strength;*
*Why do You cast me off?*
*Why do I go mourning because of the oppression*
*of the enemy?*

*~ Psalm 43:1-2*

How do you look into the eyes of a God who let you down? How do you speak the thoughts that are in your mind? Wasn't He supposed to protect us? Didn't He promise to look out for us, to keep us safe under His wing? How then did we get caught up in this event? Why? No. It is too hard to look Him in the eyes, for then all my thoughts would be revealed, and the questions would come. Could my faith endure if I opened the floodgates? It is better to keep it hidden, locked away in the deep recesses of my mind. Just carry on...

I walked those first months after 9/11 as though I was in a trance, feeling as though others led me, telling me where to go, what to do. I was afforded no consolation. My complaint remained bitter in my soul.

The groaning of my heart was not adequate to express the extent of my suffering. The grief was beyond expression. I languished in my bitterness. *Oh, that I knew where I might find Him, that I might come to His seat!* I looked, but I could not find God. When I looked to the left, I could not see Him. When I turned to the right, He was not there. Where then could my help come from if I could not find the place of God? (Job 23:1-3; 8-9) I was in the desert and God was silent. He did not speak to me for three months.

Shunned by God. Did He really turn His back on me? It seemed that way. Is this what it is to be truly alone? I felt an empty silence that followed me everywhere I went. It was like when you speak or sing in a room with poor acoustics; the sound goes out and then falls to the ground with a thud. The time between the Old Testament and the New Testament is known as the "silent years." During

> *I cry out to You,*
> *but You do not answer me;*
> *I stand up, and*
> *You regard me [not].*
> *~Job 30:20*

those four hundred years, God did not speak. There were no words spoken by inspired prophets. Nothing was written regarding the Israelites. We are left hanging, wondering if that is the end of the story. Waiting, holding our breath, for the words have left the Israelites with empty promises whose fulfillment seemed never to be accomplished. Had God said all He had to say to prepare the way for His Son? And I wondered…, why was God silent now, why had He sent me to my *silent* time?

Where was the justice, where was the help? God had thrown me into this dark place and left me standing alone. I was lost and could not find my way. Yet, where was God? Though I cried out, my words fell on deaf ears and no help came, no comfort. My life is but a shadow, already it has faded. "He breaks me down on every side, and I am gone; My hope He has uprooted like a tree." (Job 19:7-10)

I never felt anger, just a deep sense of disappointment. I told my pastor that I felt like God had let me down. He bristled then stated, "No, God did not let you down. He did protect your father, he took him to heaven. He is in a better place."

He was earnest in his reply, but defensive. It was apparent that he felt I verged on sacrilege for voicing such a thought.

I looked at him, hurt in my eyes and said, "But I need him here with me. I wasn't done with him."

It was my hurt talking. But I thought, *Why do you defend God? Does God need defending? Can He not defend Himself? Does He need us to justify His ways?*

Even so, God disappointed me. He let me down. That was how I felt. And all the defending and rationalizing would not change that fact. My intellect told me He didn't, my spirit told me He didn't, but my emotions, my hurt, my grief said He did. After all, did He not promise to protect His own? Did God not tell us in Proverbs 12:21 that "… no harm befalls the righteous, but the wicked have their fill of trouble," and in Psalm 91:11, "For He shall give His angels charge over you, to keep you in all your ways?" How then did this happen? Where was God in all this?

It was several days before September 11, 2001 that I was speaking with God, wondering what God's purpose was for my life. I felt so close to Him. I told Him to use me however He wanted, that no matter what, I would serve Him. Then disaster struck. Was this the cost of serving God? Had I truly meant what I said? Did this happen because of what I said? Job served God with unwavering faith. Tragedy struck him because of his faith. For it was the Lord who approached Satan, saying, "Have you considered my servant Job? See, there is none on earth like him. He is a blameless and upright man, who fears the Lord and shuns evil."

Satan answered the Lord and said, "Why would he not love and serve You? You have placed a hedge about him, around his household, and around all that he has. Nothing bad happens to him. You have given Job much; you have blessed him and caused him to prosper in the land. Job has not faced the trials of life as others have."

Satan paused as a smile spread across his face, "Consider this, how shall Your man Job endure if You were to stretch out Your hand against him? *Let* me touch all that is his, and he will curse You to Your face!"

Then the Lord relented and said, "Behold, all that he has is in your power. Do all that you desire, only do not take his life." (Job 1: 8-12)

> *When I lie down, I say,*
> *"When shall I arise,*
> *And the night be ended?"*
> *For I have had my fill of*
> *tossing till dawn.*
> *-Job 7:4*

What if I had not surrendered my life to God, might this not have happened to me?

Is not this life of ours a hard lot? We come upon the earth to fulfill some purpose, appointed for a time to walk upon a difficult path. We are born to suffer the trials of this world, and then we fade into oblivion. In weariness, we traverse the fields of sorrow, and then quickly we are taken away. And where do we find relief. "How long will You look away from me?… Have I sinned? What have I done to You, O watcher of men? Why do You set me as a Your target, so that I am a burden to myself?" (Job 7: 19-20)

In discussing the loss of my father with some friends at church, a dear man said to me, "Do not worry, when you fall, God is there to pick you up." I could not help myself. I did not desire to hurt this well-meaning friend, but I had to say what I felt.

"Yes, but God could have also prevented me from falling."

Silence followed. What could anyone say? I make people uncomfortable. When you are in the throes of grief, people tend to back away from you. When they find out that I lost my father on September 11, they don't know what to do. Some change the subject, some cry, others look at me in shock. I don't blame them. I do not know if I would know how to handle the situation if it were reversed. And really, what comfort is there in words. They don't change anything. Just cry with me, hold me, sit quietly by my side.

We always pray for "God's watch care over us." What does that mean? Does that mean He will protect us from harm? Then when bad things happen, when harm comes our way, did God abandon us? Can we say as Job did, "Who among all these does not know that the hand of the Lord has done this, in whose hand is the life of every living thing, and the breath of all mankind?" (Job 12:9-10)

"Oh, Lord," I cry, "lift me, lift me up. I am burdened with such a care. It is such a weight bearing down upon me, pressing me 'til my bones will break. Lift me up, hold me up, keep me in your arms. The burden crushes me until I fall, I cannot stand without Your help. Where are You?"

*How long, O Lord? Will you forget me forever? How long will you hide your face from me? How long must I wrestle with my thoughts and every day have sorrow in my heart?*
~ Psalm 13:1-2 (NIV)

Though God was silent, the American people were not. It was as if a band of brothers rose to lift us up. Those flags, those beautiful flags fluttering in the breeze, they were everywhere: lining streets, hanging from buildings and houses and overpasses. It was as though some hidden national pride awakened after the terrorists' attacks. Solidarity. We Americans may fight among ourselves like siblings, but don't mess with one of us or you will have to deal with all of us.

My father was a patriot. Often a tear could be seen tracing a path down his cheek when the national anthem was played. Forever the flag, those beautiful stars and stripes, will be etched into my mind as a symbol of loss, of freedom, of pride.

> Flags flying, bold stripes of red and white,
> Brilliant stars of freedom's might,
> Remind us all that freedom is
> Bought with a precious price.

The terrible acts on September 11 demonstrate that freedom is not guaranteed. How fragile we hold it, knowing that its loss is but one generation away. We must never forget all who have sacrificed so much down through the ages, and those yet paying for our freedoms still.

Yet, when the cost is placed upon your own life, it is hard to bear. As we think upon the evil that runs rampant in this world, it is easy to rise up and cry out, "Why God?" just as the prophet Habakkuk did as the Babylonian army marched on Jerusalem in 605 BC. There Habakkuk looked out from the wall of the city and saw the forces of Babylon encircling Jerusalem. Already, other cities had fallen in defeat to Nebuchadnezzar's strength. Despair filled his heart as he raised his voice to heaven and cried, "O LORD, how long shall I cry, and You will not hear? Even cry out to You, 'Violence!' and You will not save." (Habakkuk 1:2)

Long had the prophet called out to God, yet no change, no help had come. God's eyes are too pure to look upon evil, the very sight of it is an abomination to Him, and He must turn away. Yet, here He looks upon those who commit evil and says nothing as the righteous are devoured. (Habakkuk 1:13) How can this be? Has God abused His patience at the expense of the righteous, the innocent? Is He not a just God?

Yet, all I can do is wait. There are no answers, no comfort, just silent waiting, frozen in place, looking into the darkness.

> I dreamed I saw a great wave, climbing over green lands and above the hills. I stood upon the brink. It was utterly dark in the abyss before my feet. A light shone behind me, but I could not turn. I could only stand there, waiting.
>
> ~ *The Return of the King*[1]

Tolkien lent this vision to one of his characters in his novel, *The Lord of the Rings*. Though Tolkien here writes of his own personal nightmare, it speaks of how helpless I feel, for I stand on the brink, darkness before me, and I can do nothing to help myself. The great author reveals that "it always ends by surrender, and I awake gasping out of deep water."[2] Yet, is that not a light shining over my shoulder? Does not that light put darkness into shadow? My vision remains fixed on the darkness before me, but I can feel the glow of that light upon my back.

# Episode 5

# SEEKING AFTER HIS SHEEP

*Call to Me, and I will answer you,*
*and show you great and mighty things,*
*which you do not know.*

*~Jeremiah 33:3*

For others, they grow and change, life moves on. Change is inevitable, and life proceeds with a rhythm that sustains our doings. Slowly, the flags rose to full staff or were removed from buildings altogether. The rush of life picked up its pace as most people returned to the mode of existence they once had. Yet, I seemed to be stuck in the moment, fastened to the loss of September 11, 2001, unable to move forward. For me, time stood still. To give up the grief would be to lose that last remnant of my father. So I lingered in my sorrow, holding on so not to let go of what remained.

> *Oh, that my grief were fully weighed,*
> *And my calamity laid with it on the scales!*
> *For then it would be heavier than the sand of the sea—*
> *~ Job 6:2-3*

Grief is a lonely place to dwell. There is no one on earth who knows exactly what you are going through. Each person must experience the sorrow him or herself. It is not something you can divvy up and share. The burden is fully yours. The pain reaches me, even as I sit here. It is as though something heavy is pressing on my chest. At times, the ache is unbearable. I am often overcome by a restless agitation, unable to concentrate. So I pace, as though I can walk off the pain. I grow quiet and turn inward, lost in my thoughts. I felt fragile after September 11, like a glass teetering on the edge of a table. All it would take was a little tremor, and I would plummet to the ground, shattering into a million pieces. I needed someone to reach out and pull me back to the safety of the center of the table.

Now, as the light shines back upon my memory, I realize that the first time God reached out to me was on the morning of September 11, 2001. It began as a beautiful fall day, the air fresh, the sun warm, and the skies clear. As always, the children and I began our day with Bible study. The morning's subject was Shadrach, Meshach, and Abednego. (Daniel 3) In discussing the three who were placed into the fiery furnace for their unwavering faith in God, I made the cryptic statement that no matter what happens in our life, even when we go through the fiery furnace, still we must follow the Lord. I did not know at that very moment that my own life would be put through the furnace and my words tested. The time was 8:40 a.m. Central Time. Flight 77 crashed into the Pentagon at 9:37 a.m. Eastern Time. Was God preparing me for what would come?

A few days later, as I was with my family in Virginia dealing with the aftermath of terror, words began to flow through my mind. "There is a river that flows from God above. /There is a fountain, that's filled with His great love. /Come to the water, there is a vast supply. /There is a river, that never shall run dry."[1] It was a song, one I did not recognize. How could I know the melody and words to a song I had never before heard? But there

39

it was, streaming through my mind. I could not get it out. The song was with me the entire day, flowing freely through my thoughts and with me through my tears. I had no choice but to stop and listen. As I look back, I can see how God was reaching out to me, as a Shepherd who seeks after His lost sheep.

Water, water in dry places. I was in the desert, and here God offered me water, yet I could not see it. The hurt blinded me. I could not see His hand reaching down from above. He was offering me an endless stream of living water, clean, and fresh, and pure—water that would satisfy my wounded soul, not stale water that had been stored in a cistern, green with algae and waste. But water that is renewed daily as the stream flows down from above. All I need do was come. (John 4:14) Yet, I could not find my way. I could not understand the call.

> *If anyone is thirsty, let him come to me and drink. Whoever believes in me, as the Scripture has said, streams of living water will flow from within him.*
> ~ John 7:37-38 (NIV)

All these long years, I have felt that my family lived under a golden star of protection. In fact, several people have told us this. The evidence of the past has borne this belief as we have seen time and again how God has taken us out of danger and kept us safe. Once on vacation, as we stopped to get gas, my father noticed a bubble on one of our tires. He worried this could lead to a blowout. In order to prevent any danger, we bought a new tire.

With new tire on and our hearts thrilled with excitement to continue our vacation, we once more started down the road. Yet, something caused my father to pull over and look at our tires. Another tire had a bubble in it. So we turned the car around and headed back for another tire. Now, two new tires and several hours later, we ventured on the road once more. Traffic began to slow. We approached what looked like the remains of an accident. We all gasped in disbelief. Flattened on the side of the road was a green station wagon just like ours. An 18-wheeler had crushed the car. None of us questioned what had happened. God had intervened. It could have been us if not for the delays.

Whenever we were delayed or became lost, my father would always say, "We are here because we are *supposed* to be here." My father had not planned to take that flight to California that day. It was only a few days before September 11 that his intentions changed. He had originally been scheduled to attend a meeting in Virginia, but he told my mother that the trip to California "would be more interesting." Was my father *supposed* to be on that plane? Why had God always protected us before, but not this time? He had always taken us out of harm's way, not put us into it. It was not in my frame of reference that the Lord would not always protect any member of my family from harm. Then the phone rang and my world came crashing in on me.

I am now looking back from the end of the tunnel, or at least close enough to the end to see the light. It was not always so. When I first entered the tunnel, there was no visible light, only darkness and grief. Out of the shadow, the Enemy spoke, crushing me with his words, saying, "Where is your God?" (Psalm 42:10) Dejected and forsaken of God, the thought tormented my soul. But why, "Why are you cast down, O my soul? And why are you disquieted within me? Hope in God." *Oh, God, manifest Your presence to me; give light to my path that I may see Your face.* I stay myself upon my God, "for I shall yet praise Him, the help of my countenance and my God," the true source of my comfort. (Psalm 42:11)

Yet, how could God allow this terrible thing to happen to our family? To my father who was so good? "We are Your children. If You are so good, why?"

I continued my relationship with God. I prayed. However, I never broached the topic of September 11. I could not read the Bible. I could not look into His eyes. If I looked into His eyes, I would have to face the questions and disappointments. He would see into my eyes as well, and I would not be able to hide my thoughts and feelings from Him. I could not hide my disappointment in my God who had let me down, this God who was supposed to be my protector and shield. Was that not His promise to us as His children, to love and protect us? Yet somehow, my father had been led to his death.

If I thought about God's hand upon the events, if I voiced what was in my heart, may it be that my faith in God would waver? Then I might miss out. I had an investment now in heaven, and I did not want to miss it. So for months, God was silent, because I would not hear Him. I would not listen. I would not question. I would not see. It was safer that way, it was better.

Of course, He already knew my hurts and doubts. He knew my sorrow, but He could not reach me, because I would not look up. So He reached across to me with an unlikely source.

December of 2001, my husband took me to see Peter Jackson's cinematic rendition of Tolkien's *The Fellowship of the Ring*. Seeing this movie was supposed to take my mind off the thought that the following week we would be laying my father's remains to rest, three months after September 11. God spoke to me through the movie trilogy *The Lord of the Rings*. He spoke to me across time through the words of J. R. R. Tolkien. Was it just by chance that the film *The Fellowship of the Ring* came out that December? Or was there a Greater Power at work?

As I sat in the theater, I assumed I was about to watch an adventure drama geared more to men than to me. I sat there amazed. As the Fellowship entered into the Mines of Moria, Frodo, the main protagonist of the story, who being an unlikely candidate to hold the future of Middle Earth in his hands, confronted Gandalf, the wise old leader of the group, with tough questions, the questions I had avoided bringing before God. It was surreal. As he spoke, the audience in the theater melted away. It was only Gandalf looking at me as a beam of light leapt off the screen, alighting me in its illumination, a tunnel between the screen and myself, as though no one else was in the room. Frodo stated to Gandalf, "I wish this had never happened, I wish the ring had never come to me."[2]

Gandalf looked full upon me, his eyes boring into my very soul as though the words written by Tolkien fifty years earlier were written for me. "So do all who live to see such times. But that is not for them to decide, all we have to decide is what to do with the time that is given to us."[3]

I was jarred to the core. It seemed so simple. Yes, that is all I have to do. God had spoken to me through Tolkien, reaching out to me to address the issue at hand. When I would run from the dispute, He sought me out, taking me by the hand in His overwhelming Love. It all began to make sense. God had not really let me down. A great weight lifted from my shoulders and I began to look up. My ears began to hear the voice of God. I do not have the power to change what had happened… all I can do is go forward. I did not have control over what occurred on

September 11. However, I do have control of how I respond to it. This is all I must decide. But how do I go on from here?

Suddenly, I could see how God had been speaking to me all along. The floodgates now opened, and I drew in water that filled my soul with wonder. But there was still work to be done. I started asking God those tough questions. I sought out the answers. I devoured all the works I could find of Tolkien to see if there was more in the pages of his books to help me understand this God of mine. And most importantly, I began to read God's word with new eyes, eyes that looked Him directly in the face, unencumbered by the shadow of fear.

> O LORD, I have heard Your speech and was afraid;
> O LORD, revive Your work in the midst of the years!
> In the midst of the years make it known;
> In wrath remember mercy.
> - Habakkuk 3:2

Then I remembered a dream I had in the fall of 2001. Not every dream had been bad. I dreamt I was sitting at a table across from my father. Someone else sat beside him, yet I could not make out the man's face. I did not question the identity of this person. It was as though I knew who he was and why he was there. My sense was that the man was my father's guardian angel. It seemed only natural that the unknown person was present.

"Are you happy?" I asked my father.

"Yes, I am very happy," he calmly replied.

As I looked at my father, I could not help but notice that his eyes were no longer brown, but a deep blue. In my dream I thought, *they are blue, deep blue, like a lake you could jump into.*

My father leaned toward me and said, "Take care of your mother."

"I will," I responded.

Leaning closer, he continued, "I can show you where to find my body, but you cannot tell your mother."

Next, my dream took me to a neighborhood, one that I had not seen before. I was walking with my mother down a sidewalk along a street lined with stone retaining walls. The neighborhood reminded me of some of the older ones in Virginia. The houses were temple-front Greek revival cottages and Tudor bungalows, styles popular in the mid-1920s and early 1930s with broad stairs leading up to the front doors.

We were walking side by side, my mother and me, down a slight grade. As we walked, the stone retaining wall grew taller beside us as the road sloped downward. I remember telling my mother of the dream I was having while I was still in the dream. Then I woke. I felt as though I had had a visitation from my father. The impression of spending time in his presence overwhelmed me. My grief spilled over into tears. Not long after we received word from the FBI that they had identified my father's remains.

That December of 2001, we laid my father to rest. We buried him on a hill in the Garden of Time under a dogwood tree. It was an icy cold day, the wind whipped across our faces, biting us as the tears flowed. As the hearse drove into view, the finality of my father's death settled upon me. The evidence stood before me. The flag-draped casket was carried from the hearse to the waiting grave. The numbness of shock had worn off. The full force of grief hit us as the brief service concluded at the graveside. A few words were spoken, then we were quickly

*As a shepherd seeks out his flock on the day he is among his scattered sheep, so will I seek out My sheep and deliver them from all the places where they were scattered on a cloudy and dark day.*
*- Ezekiel 34:12*

whisked away to shield us from the cold. As I went to get into the car, I turned and looked again at the casket. Too fast it had been. I didn't feel as if I had really said good-bye. Maybe it was because the burial had not been preceded by a church service. We all felt hollow and unsatisfied. I felt as though I had been living a funeral for three months and now it was over, and I did not know how to go on from there. The journey was not over. I still had a long way to trod. Yet, I knew that God would be with me, for He had sought me out and I had found Him.

# Episode 6

# THROUGH THE VEIL

*Let not your heart be sad,*
*though night must follow noon,*
*and already our evening draweth nigh.*
*~J. R. R. Tolkien*[1]

Growing weary of the multitudes that pressed against Him, Jesus departed from the crowd taking with him Peter, James, and John. With some effort, He led them up the side of a high mountain apart from the people below. The day was waning. The sky glowed golden in the West, reaching out its arms as though clinging to the last of day as the shadow of night closed across the aerial plain. Fatigue weighed heavy upon the four men as they reached the summit of the mountain. Together they looked out across the vast expanse, the beauty of the land stretched before them as the last rays of light lingered. Then Jesus went off to pray, a solitary figure kneeling as the shade of night silhouetted His form in shadow.

Now, Peter and the two who were with him, being weary, were heavy with sleep. As their eyes began to fail, just as they had lain down wrapped in a torpid somnolence, something seized them, rousing them fully awake. Looking up, with eyes wide open, they beheld a sight beyond apprehension. Before them stood the glory of Jesus, shining white, like snow glistening on the mountainside. His countenance changed, yet somehow the same, shone with radiant glory streaming from His face. It was as though day struck the mountaintop as the full power of the sun shone upon it. He did not stand alone, but two stood with Him, and they appeared to them as Elijah and Moses, dead yet alive again, talking with Jesus concerning matters that were to come.

While they were still speaking, behold, a bright cloud overspread them, filling the vision with a mighty power. Suddenly, a voice, full of greatness and glory, came out of the cloud, saying, "This is My beloved Son. Hear Him!" the sound of which caused Peter, James, and John to fall down upon their faces for they were greatly afraid. There was a stillness in the air. Softly, a hand rested on the men as Jesus reached out and touched His disciples.

"Arise," spoke Jesus gently, "and do not be afraid."

Looking up at the touch of the Master, the men lifted their eyes and saw Jesus only. (Matthew 17:1-8)

Now the king of Syria had in his mind to go against Israel to make war upon the city. Knowing that Elisha, the prophet of God, was providing information to the king of Israel, the king of Syria sent out horses and chariots and a great army and they came by night and surrounded the city. When Elisha rose early the next morning and went out upon the wall, behold, there was the army of Syria surrounding the city with a whole host of men, and horses, and chariots.

Elisha's servant gasped beside him at the sight, saying, "Alas, my master! What shall we do?"

Elisha looked at his servant, smiled, and then answered him, "Do not fear, for those who are with us are more than those who are with them."

The servant bent his head to the side and looked in wonder at the prophet, not understanding his speech. Elisha raised his voice to heaven and prayed, "Lord, I pray, open his eyes that he may see."

Suddenly, the eyes of the servant were opened, and the young man saw with his own eyes and he was amazed, for upon the mountain a host of angelic beings stood, full of horses and chariots of fire all around. (2 Kings 6:8-17)

Many stories are told, like these from the scriptures; glimpses beyond our present world. Like gossamer threads floating upon the air in fair weather, it is but a thin veil that separates this corporal world and the next. How easily a soul slips from this sphere into the land beyond the veil. One breath is all that stands between this life we know and the far country that is to be our home. Are we truly cut off from those behind the veil, or can we glimpse, if only in shadow, the images behind the curtain? A delicate velum flowing gently between this world and the next, it seems, can be lightly brushed aside bringing into focus that which was hidden. And there are those who have been permitted a glimpse of it.

The first time I experienced this fleeting image beyond the curtain of this world was when I was working as an oncology nurse on the nightshift. We recently had several deaths on our floor. My fellow nursing staff and I were sitting at the nurse's desk working on charts. The dark hallways were quiet as patients slept and the bustle of the day rested. Suddenly, we all started in our seats. The semblance of a shadowy figure cast upon our peripheral vision set our hearts apace and brought us to our feet. In a singular cohesive movement, each of us turned to the same hallway.

"Did you see that?" one asked.

We all nodded in affirmation. Wide-eyed we looked into one another's faces, and then we hurried to check on our patients. No one was taken that night, but we all knew we had seen the shadow of the Angel of Death walk the halls that night. None of us ever questioned what had happened.

When my oldest son was a small child, around three years old, we were visiting my mother and father in Virginia. We were all sitting in the living room talking when we noticed that my son was looking up in the corner of the ceiling talking to someone. In amazement, we watched.

When his conversation was over, I asked him, "Who were you talking to?" He shrugged his shoulders. I asked him what the object of his conversation looked like. I had with me a copy of the magazine *Angels on Earth*. My son came over to where I sat and pointed to a picture of an angel and said, "Like that."

There was one other time my son was having a discussion with someone I could not see. He was outside riding in his little car when he suddenly got out, shut the car door, and began an animated conversation with an invisible being. When it was over, he got back into the car and drove away. In jest, we spoke of my son having secret meetings with his guardian angels. Being quite active and at times careless, my son has often been saved from harm at just the last moment, keeping his angels very busy. Perhaps my son was addressing his angel. It is often believed that children are able to see through the veil of this world to the next more readily than adults can. Maybe it is because they are not tainted with the

> *For He shall give His angels charge over you, To keep you in all your ways. In their hands they shall bear you up, Lest you dash your foot against a stone.*
> *- Psalm 91:11-12*

skepticism that age brings.

These instances happened prior to September 11, 2001, opening a door to my acceptance of the mysteries that surround us. So it was not difficult to believe as members of my family began telling of their otherworldly experiences following the death of my father.

We stayed in Virginia for two and a half weeks after September 11, 2001. But as life will have it, we had to return to our home and pick up the threads of our existence. The morning after we had all left my mother's house, my mother told us she awoke in the dark of the early morning. She had sensed a presence above her. As she opened her eyes, she saw the silhouette of a man leaning over her. At first, she thought it was my husband checking in on her, but then she realized we had left. When she understood clearly that she was all alone in the house, she gasped, and the shadow vanished. She said the image reminded her of my father's physique when he was in his thirties. Could this have been the spirit of my father checking on my mother?

Soon after September 11, my sister was sitting at her kitchen table doing paperwork when she felt a presence walk behind her. She turned to look, but no one was there. The feeling passed. She felt certain it was our father telling her everything would be okay, that he was still with us. For her, this was a reassurance that he was well, that she had no need to worry or grieve over his death. Everything would be okay.

Missing my father's presence, my mother asked my father if he could hear her, and that if he were able, would he give her a sign. It was then that the alarm clock in my brother's old bedroom began sounding off at ten o'clock every morning. My mother would go down to the room, turn it off, and then make sure the alarm was not set. It hadn't been, yet the next day, the alarm went off again. This went on for quite some time, becoming a nuisance instead of a reassurance. As the intensity of loss lessened, and my mother resumed a semblance of normalcy in her life, the alarm stopped sounding.

In May of 2002, my mother and I were at the airport awaiting a flight to attend my brother's graduation from Eastman University. We had to leave the gate where we were sitting so bomb-sniffing dogs could search the area. When we returned to our seats, we saw two pennies on the floor in front of the chairs in which we had been sitting. My mother reached down and picked them up, saying they were pennies from heaven. She told me she had a collection of them; that this had been happening often since September 11. My mother said she had been finding pennies lying around in unexpected places seemingly appearing out of nowhere.

With the approach of my parents' forty-fourth wedding anniversary on June 14, 2002, my mother shared with me that she greatly missed my father. She wished he would communicate with her again. When she awoke on the morning of their anniversary, she felt the presence of hands on the small of her back as though someone had arms around her. She felt this the entire day. As night fell, the hands left her.

My brother wed in May of 2003, another milestone missed by my father. At the wedding, off to the side near the altar, stood a Remembrance Candle, a symbol of the presence of our father's spirit. My brother walked our mother down the aisle and stopped to light the candle. As they did, the flame flared up brightly as if our father's spirit hovered over the flame, breathing life into it. The flame remained liberal in size and lavished its brightness throughout the service. Life lived in that candle beyond the expectation of the customary glow.

My father had a theory regarding time and eternity. In jest, he stated that all of us are already within the folds of eternity; we just don't know it yet. His theory was based on Einstein's Special Theory of Relativity. This theory basically states that the speed at which time travels is relative to where you are experiencing time. In other words, time within the bounds of eternity is slower than time as it is experienced on earth. What feels to us as years, may be as seconds to those beyond the veil. Thus, we are already there, but don't know it. There is a certain comfort for us in this thought, however far-fetched it may be. When we enter beyond the curtain of this world, time will slow and what may seem to those left behind as a very long separation, to us who venture on, it will be but a blink of the eye until we are reunited.

There is a hope beyond the veil that life does not end. The glimpses afforded many attest to the affirmation that life exists outside the bounds of this present world, that we are not alone. An active spiritual world exists apart from what we see and know, that runs, not parallel, but tangent to our world. This gives us hope in an eternal home where one day we will reunite with those who have gone on before us. Death is not the end, but a transition.

> *This hope we have as an anchor of the soul, both sure and steadfast, and which enters the Presence behind the veil.*
> *~ Hebrews 6:19*

As the veil is lifted off the face of mourning so too God will brush aside the covering, which is cast over all people. On that day, we shall see with our eyes all that has transpired with a vision unencumbered, for the Lord will take away the veil that covers our faces, and grief will hinder us no more. (Isaiah 25:7-8)

# Episode 7

# SILENT RESOLVE

*He will not be afraid of evil tidings;*
*His heart is steadfast, trusting in the LORD.*

*~ Psalm 112:7*

He was our anchor, holding fast our family, the mainstay of our domesticity, firmly fixing and stabilizing our bearings. He was our emblem of hope. Without him, our ship was adrift, floundering on a turbulent sea. If ever we needed my father, it was in those first few months after September 11. Maybe we needed him too much. Perhaps we needed to learn to depend more on God. Could it be that it was because of whom he was, how good a man he was, that my father was taken? He was spared the decline and disability of age. Maybe he was preserved from something worse down the road. I suppose we will never know. May it be that the "why" doesn't matter as much as what has happened to us who remain behind. Is there something within the character and life of my father that can bring comfort and guidance to us now?

One of my father's coworkers was the last person we know to have seen him alive. He told us he saw my father sitting at the gate waiting for his flight. He was drinking coffee and working on his laptop. The coworker said a few words of greeting then left to board his own flight. That was typical Daddy, a cup of coffee and his laptop. In fact, he had been working all weekend on a design for a new airplane that Raytheon was developing. Excitement about the prospect of continuing his efforts with his colleagues in Goleta, California, was what brought him to his decision to change plans and take Flight 77 on September 11.

And so, my father's life ended at the Pentagon in Arlington, Virginia, not far from where it had begun. He was born on April 14, 1933, in his parent's little house in Arlington. He attended Washington Lee High School. Then in 1953, at the age of twenty, my father was drafted into the army and served for two years during the Korean War. My father desired to enter the service as a conscientious objector. In good faith, he could not say that he would not defend his family from intruders; therefore, though uncomfortable with the idea of taking another's life, he was willing to fight for the security of his country against tyranny and foreign invasion. He spent the rest of his life dedicated to the defense of his beloved country.

Throughout the course of the war, my father remained stateside, often hanging out of helicopters to photograph the land below in order to convert the information gathered into maps. It was during his time in the service that he was exposed to engineering and developed a passion for this field of interest. Taking advantage of the GI bill, he entered college where he studied electrical engineering. He married Judie Marie Whitener on June 14, 1958, ironically on Flag Day (since forever the American flag will be a reminder of 9/11). She was a nineteen-year-old daughter of a barber, he a twenty-five-year-old student.

After graduating from George Washington University in 1959 with a Bachelor of Science in Engineering, the couple moved to Baltimore, Maryland, where my father began working for the

Martin Company, participating in various projects such as the Titan Missile program. By the time the couple had one daughter, Jane Marie, born to them on March 11, 1960, my father decided to further his education, earning a master's degree from Drexel University in 1963. With his career well underway, the couple added a second daughter, this author, Susan Lynn, on May 5, 1964. Our family moved to a little house in the woods outside of Baltimore in the fall of 1964, where my father began working for the Bunker Ramo Cooperation in White Oak, Maryland. As America prepared to place the first man on the moon, my parents brought forth their only son, Randall Burgess on April 9, 1969.

In October of 1971, our family transferred to Westlake, California, where my father continued working for the Bunker Ramo Cooperation. My father was responsible for system design and testing of passive Electrical Warfare (EW) systems, active and passive sonar systems, and data management systems for the United States Army. He taught EW classes at Point Mugu Naval Air Station and later at Raytheon in Goleta, California. With this job came the beginning of several moves back and forth across the country, with the Department of Defense's (DOD) encouragement, as my father worked on various DOD contracts.

We moved back to the East Coast in December of 1979, where my father worked for the Litton Company in College Park, Maryland. There he was Technical Director of Advanced Programs, working on receiver/processor technology and the AN/ALQ-99 Advanced Capabilities for EA-6B and EF-111A aircraft. Often, he spent time at the Pentagon working alongside the DOD, speaking to Congress regarding defense contracts, building up a reputation of distinction and integrity. The year 1983 brought another move as we returned to California where my father began his job with Hughes Aircraft Radar Systems Group, in El Segundo. While at Hughes Aircraft, which later merged with Raytheon, my father helped develop and build antiradar technology.

In 1995, my parents left the West Coast and returned to Virginia so my father could work at Raytheon's Washington, DC facility where he was the director of program management. Projects my father was involved in at Raytheon included the "EW/radar shared aperture and digital receiver electronics. He conceived Raytheon's AN/ALR-67(V)3 next generation radar warning receiver for US Navy F/A-18E/F aircraft. He also made valuable contributions to the development of standoff jammer, digital RF memory, and emitter location technologies."[1]

His reputation was of an industry expert in receiver technology. He helped pioneer tactical use of interfero-meters, high speed A/D conversion, and techniques used for signal feature extraction, and he led the charge for practical use of channelized receiver technology. Deemed "the Father of Electronic Warfare," he contributed to just about every EW system in use today, holding many patents for his conceptions. All his work focused on the protection of US and allied military forces.[2]

> We are remembering Stanley as a hero to the United States of America.
> ~ Gari Cross, Waco, TX

As the nation collectively began to mourn, thoughtful gifts came streaming in. The country's leaders began envisioning ways to honor those who contributed to our nation's security. On November 13, 2001, my father was awarded the Defense of Freedom Medal by Army Brigadier General Edward M. Harrington, director of the Defense Contract Management Agency, on behalf of President Bush. Equivalent to the Purple

Heart for non-military personnel, this medal recognizes civilian Department of Defense employees killed on September 11, 2001.

To honor the accomplishments and mentorship my father brought to EW, the Association of Old Crows (AOC) established the Stanley R. Hall Business Development Award. This award is presented in my father's name for "exceptional accomplishments in fostering a positive position for EW/IS and enhancing the existing business base of the recipient's organization." The AOC, which my father had been a member for as long as I can remember, is a national forum for sharing ideas and experiences in the EW community. The AOC continues to honor my father for "devoting over forty years of his life to the pursuit of peace and the protection of US Air Force, Navy, and Army forces."[3]

Raytheon dedicated a lab in their Goleta, California, office in my father's name. This is the facility to which he was journeying on that fateful day. My mother and I attended the dedication ceremony where we were treated with great gentility. It was heartwarming to talk with coworkers who loved and respected

Mr. Hall typified the finest of our nation's engineering professionals; he was a true gentleman, quiet, unassuming, absolutely competent, and a man of great personal integrity and honor. He loved his job immensely, but perhaps his most important contribution was his commitment to the young engineers he mentored. Numerous engineers within Raytheon and his former employers have thrived under his tutelage. By sharing his gift for engineering through his teaching and personal relationships, his legacy will continue for years to come. He will be remembered for his pioneering spirit, warm heart, and strong sense of patriotism. (AOC)[4] my father. Also amazing was to see inside the professional life of my father. He never talked much at home about his job. We stood proud of him that day and with a better understanding of the personal sacrifices he made for the betterment of our nation.

As we attended the events at the Pentagon or the White House, a master sergeant accompanied each victim's family members. Every memorial service and remembrance was performed with dignity and distinction, our servicemen and servicewomen honoring us with their hallowed dedication to our family and our country. As word spread of our loss, gifts and well wishes flooded in. We received letters of condolence from all across the world, from Madrid, Spain, to Milton, Florida. People reached out to us in our national and personal pain. Mercy bands in memory of those lost on 9/11 were distributed. Many who wore my father's name sent heartfelt condolences. It was all overwhelming.

The September 11, Victim Compensation Fund was established in an attempt to recompense victims and their families. As the daughter of a 9/11 victim, I had to send an affidavit affirming the monetary value of my father's loss. How can you measure a person's worth in dollars? No amount of money could ease the loss we felt. Each victim of September 11 was worth so much more. Those whose lives were cut short before they had a chance to live were just as valuable to their families as those well established in society were.

When I was in grade school, I had to write a small piece describing whom I thought was a great person in the world. I could have chosen anyone: a sports figure, a movie star, a person in history. Instead, I wrote, "My father, because he loves me and he is nice. I love my father. When I need help he helps me."

Whenever I needed help with homework, I often ventured downstairs to my father's office. He was always willing to stop his own work to come to my aid. Often I desired his assistance in achieving the solution to one particular math problem, but he would go into a long dissertation attempting to lead me to understand the reasoning behind the mathematical operation. I would grow impatient, wanting to get on with it so I could just finish my homework and move on to more interesting pursuits. Nonetheless, he would continue until I had a solid grasp of the concept.

When I had questions about the Bible or God, my father would never just come out and provide me with direct answers. He would put on that crooked smile of his, lean back in his chair, and point to his bookshelf. "The answer can be found in one of these books," he would say. I would sigh, my shoulders slumping, wanting quick answers. Then I would search his library until I found what I needed to resolve my query.

Now, as I look back, I am so thankful for the instruction he gave me. I have spent my life seeking answers to questions, desiring to learn and understand. Research has become my passion. Really, I could spend all day researching any number of topics. I credit my father for this love of learning that I now possess. What I saw as a frustration when I was teenager, I cherish now as a gift. And so, I pass the teaching on to my children. I see the same frustration in their eyes, and I smile and thank God that I was blessed to have the father that I had.

When I was seven years old, my family and I went on vacation to Ocracoke Island, North Carolina. We rented a cute little cottage and planned to spend a pleasant week at the beach. At the time, my father worked for the Bunker Ramo Corporation in White Oak, Maryland. Shortly after arriving in North Carolina, my father received a call that some desperate need had arisen at work and his presence was required. We drove my father to an airfield where a helicopter landed, picked him up, and took him away. My siblings and I found this amazing. He was gone for some time, leaving my mother with three small children on an island.

We never took a vacation where my father didn't pull over to a pay phone to check in at the office. We would sit in the car and wait impatiently for him to return. It seemed his office could not survive without him; a feeling well understood by us today as we struggle to live without his presence to sustain us.

My father liked to travel, taking us all over this great country. We would often go to museums where he patiently read to us all the information at every exhibit so we could share in the knowledge and history of each place. When I was in elementary school, I could answer many of the teacher's questions before the topic was discussed.

My classmates would ask me, "How did you know that?"

I would respond that I saw it in a museum during one of our travels. I do believe those trips awakened something in me that to this day pulls me toward a need to learn all I can, to connect to a time and place in history. One trip my father always wished to take, but never had the opportunity, was to retrace the journey of Lewis and Clark from start to finish. I hope that one day I can make that journey in his stead.

At times, we would find ourselves traveling by car at night. The three of us children would lie down in the backseat. As I rested in that place between wake and sleep, the soft sound of my parents talking filled me with a sense of security that assured me I was safe as long as they were there.

I remember when we lived in Westlake, California, waking up to the sun filtering through the window of my bedroom. My window was open, as it often was, filling the room with the wholesome morning air, the kind of air that takes you out of yourself. The sound of the pool filter humming met me as I rejoined the waking world. It was a warm, comforting sound. I would look out my window and see my father working on the filter or cleaning the pool. How safe I felt knowing my father was always there.

He was a safe harbor. There was something in my father that spoke of assurance and power. Was it his booming bass voice, his brilliant intellect, or his calm demeanor? Yet, when my mother would ask me to call my father to dinner, my stomach would quake and my heart would flutter. I would stand outside my father's closed office door and work up the courage to knock. Of what was I afraid? I do not know. My father never did anything to make me feel that way. He was simply larger than life.

His very presence was overwhelming. Apparently, I was not alone in that feeling. When we first attended a church in Rockville, Maryland, a member of the congregation walked up to us in the parking lot. He reached out his hand to shake the hand of my father. As he introduced himself, he inquired if my father was a senator. There my father stood

... he was able to bring forth ideas in a smiling, good natured way that made it a joy to listen to his critics, comments and corrections.... He was admired and respected. We will truly miss him not only for his brilliance, but also for his warm hearted friendship. His spirit lives on as we try to emulate him.

– Richard Tate, Goleta, CA

with his snow-white hair, arrayed in his sharp three-piece suit.

His very presence spoke of something great and important. Charles Kohnstam spoke regarding my father, "… I was a fresh new grad, and he was the feared and revered chief engineer. To me in those days, he was larger than life." Richard Hill of Waco, Texas, said, "He stood out as someone that I looked up to and enjoyed working with." Other comments sent to us regarding the character of my father included words such as "a true gentleman" and "a brilliant, wonderful, and inspirational man."

My father was a serious-minded person who, according to Roberta Gotfried, brought a "sense of humanity… to every meeting and project." He was no respecter of persons, seeing everyone as contributors, regarding each person's ideas as valuable. Fair-minded and patient, he demonstrated a spirit of respect and kind regard for all with whom he came in contact.

He was a humble man. Never did I see him put on airs or become puffed up by his own brilliance. Yet, this humility did not engender in him a sense of passivity that allowed others to sway him when he knew he stood in the right. He possessed a quiet stubbornness, which my husband will tell you I inherited, that provided him with the staunchness to stand his ground. My grandmother told me of an incident when my father's resoluteness first became apparent. When my father was quite young, he had

> … he was looked upon by his co-workers, management, and government as one of the country's preeminent experts in his field. While so many people become arrogant with such high distinction, Stan always appeared a very pleasant, humble man who was respectful of everyone's opinions, regardless of position. It is his character that sets an example for us in our jobs and our lives…
>
> - Robert Szelistowki

thrown a handkerchief upon the ground and refused to pick it up. My grandmother said they stood over that handkerchief for a considerable length of time, each one refusing to budge. Finally, my father gave in to the wishes of his mother and picked up the handkerchief. This stubbornness grew into a resolve to live his life with integrity, despite the pressures and trials of life.

With hard work and tenacity, he believed all situations could have a favorable outcome. Though often shy with people, his affable nature often overcame his feelings of bashfulness, his commanding presence covering up any evidence of his uneasiness. Favorably disposed, he was a man upon whom one could depend. Bob Lawrence of Rockville, Maryland, stated that he "… could always count on Stan for a smile, an unflappable positive attitude, and good advice." According to Don Rauch in a letter he sent the family, "… he was a low key type of fellow, always very thoughtful. From the sound of his voice on the phone, you could tell he always had a smile on his face."

Understated by design, my father maintained a firm composure under the most extreme circumstances. Though his attitude was one of restrained equanimity, he did not demonstrate a dull persona. "He… always had a twinkle in his eye and a good comment for everyone." (Sherril Hisaw Gerard)

Predominately serious in nature, my father was not without humor. When he bought his first wash and wear suit, he did just that. He wore the suit, entered the shower (still arrayed), and proceeded to wash it with a bar of soap. My mother captured this event in a photograph that I have always enjoyed gazing upon with a giggle.

When I was a child, my father would quietly sit at the kitchen table while we ate dinner. Then he would begin singing, "Daddy sang bass, Mama sang tenor," using amusing voices—the bass part in his lowest bass, the tenor voice, his best female falsetto. We would all roar with laughter. We cherished these few glimpses, for he rarely showed his lighter side.

That lighter side could be seen in other activities in my father's life. Often while doing my homework in my room, I would be interrupted by the sound of whiffle balls hitting the house. I would look out the window to see my father practicing his golf swing, his stroke aiming directly to the back of our house.

He loved convertibles. He would tool around town in his brown Oldsmobile convertible wearing his driving cap, the wind whipping through the open car.

Often my father was seen making a trek across the lawn on his riding mower, waving to the neighbors. Or walking behind his snowblower, a monstrous machine in which he took great pride. Many a weekend, he would walk through the woods behind my parent's house, tending the dogwood trees, which were highly favored in his sight. Among the trees, he labored to build a flagstone patio where he envisioned the family gathering to pick crabs. It was this patio that he worked on the weekend before September 11. With just a few stones left to place, he quit for the day, telling my mother that he would finish the job when he returned from his trip to California. He never had the chance to finish. My brother completed the task as a labor of love and remembrance. The patio stands as a symbol of my father's life unfinished.

My father spent most of his time pursuing solitary endeavors. He kept his thoughts close. When it came to emotions, expressing himself verbally was difficult. He could not initiate a hug or form the words, "I love you." As I became an adult, I decided I would hug him. At first, I found that I had difficulty initiating the hugs, but the more I pushed myself, the easier it became. Always, when he came to visit me while on business, he would linger at the door as though waiting for something. I would reach out and hug him, and then he would hug me back.

Sometimes, words are difficult. My father always said that actions speak louder than words. Though very busy with work, my father always took time to attend our music and sporting events. He was often in the role of assistant coach to our sport teams. His actions never failed to say I love you.

He could never tell us outright that he was proud of us, but we could see it on his face. On my wedding day, as I slipped my arm through my father's as he prepared to walk me down the aisle, I looked into his eyes and saw them well up with tears. I will never forget that expression. No words were necessary; his eyes said it all.

One of his coworkers sent us a letter saying that he knew my father was very proud of his family by the stories he told. Whenever my father looked upon one of his grandchildren, we could see his pride in the way his eyes twinkled when he smiled.

I would often come downstairs in the morning when visiting my parents to find my daughter sitting on her grandfather's lap while he worked at his desk. When she was little, if Grandpa was sitting at the table working, she would bring her play desk next to him and work alongside him. My oldest son had a special bond with his grandfather. They were both cut from the same cloth in looks, personality, and interests. My son would ask Grandpa to come watch him play on the computer. So my father would take his laptop and sit next to my son, each working on his own computer, side by side.

As I began having children, it soon became apparent that I had my hands full. My daughter, beautiful and sweet, was ADHD, which caused all kinds of havoc for our family: impulse control issues, hyperactivity, distractibility, mood swings. School became an ordeal for her and those around her. So in order to better serve the needs of my daughter and to get a handle on the situation, I pulled her out of school, quit my nursing job, and started homeschooling. The responsibility was overwhelming at first, though proved the best act I could have done for her. Yet, I had my difficulties, often feeling sorry for myself and full of fear for the future. I shared some of my concerns with my father, expressing my sense of disappointment.

Quietly and calmly, my father listened as I spoke. "I was a good child. I thought what goes around comes around. I did not deserve this."

When I finished talking, he stated confidently, "Maybe it is because of whom you are that this has happened. *She* needed *you* as her mother."

That simple statement changed my whole outlook. Instead of looking at the situation as something being done to me, I began to see it as a mission of love for my child. Now my daughter is almost through her college education, a beautiful and successful student with the world before her. My father always had a way of putting things into perspective.

My sister told me of a conversation she and her husband had with my father on the Labor Day before September 11, 2001 regarding the end of time. My father had said the main point to remember is that the end will come, and we just need to be sure we are ready. How profound, for within a week's time my father was taken. This was the last conversation he had with my sister's family. He often did not say much, but when he spoke, his words were thoughtful and wise.

The Christmas before September 11, 2001, was the last time I saw my father. As he was leaving, I realized that I had not taken a picture of him holding my infant son. "Oh well," I thought. "We'll get it next time." There never was a next time. He never got to know my youngest son. He met him only once when my son was three months old. Now at age eleven, my son often lowers his head to the table and cries, "I miss my Grandpa." We will probably never know why some people were saved and others were lost that day. Maybe it is not for us to know. What I do know is that God holds tomorrow, and there are no better hands to hold it than the Lord's.

My father spent much of his time studying God's word and teaching Bible study in church. He had a deep insight into spiritual matters. I have collected all his notes from years of study, hoping to preserve all the knowledge and wisdom my father provided over the years. How many people he brought to the Lord or influenced toward a more spiritual life, one cannot say. But I can say this; there was no victory for the terrorists that day. They awoke, not as promised to a paradise with seven virgins awaiting them, but to a fiery hell of torment and pain that will never cease. My father, and a multitude of others, awoke in Glory, free from pain and death. He had the victory in Christ Jesus. We were able to sing "Victory in Jesus" at the close of my father's memorial service without reservation.

"Stan spent much of his life's energy making our nation safe… Stan would want us to remember him with a smile after the tears are past." (Dick Jennings, Tucson, Arizona) The memory must not fade.

Senior picture, Washington Lee High School, June 16, 1951; U.S. Army, 1953; Newlyweds, August 1958; Wash and Wear Suit, 1958

Daddy and his girls, late 1960's; Receiving an
engineering award, early 1970's

Our Family, December 1970; Our family, 1982

My wedding, January 17, 1987; Grandpa with the
grandkids, December 1996

Drawing made by my six year old son in response to 9/11

# Episode 8

# THE FACE OF EVIL

*The LORD shall preserve you from all evil;*
*He shall preserve your soul.*
*The LORD shall preserve your going out and*
*your coming in*
*From this time forth, and even forevermore.*
*~ Psalms 121: 7-8*

Every time I think I am climbing out of the pit of despair, I slip back in, drowning. It does not end. It never ends. C. S. Lewis saw grief as a spiral, or at least he hoped it was a spiral and not a circle, for there is to a certain degree of hope in a spiral.[1]

The problem with a spiral is that when the force of your momentum lessens, gravity takes hold of you, and you begin to slip back down until you can get a firm footing and climb up again. When I think about the trauma of September 11, my heart flutters, and the bottom of my stomach falls. There are so many triggers: the number 911, the American flag, the word terrorists, or Islam, the symbol for the Pentagon, or when the clock reads 9:11. (Why is it that I always see 9:11 on the clock now? Did I see it before and never noticed?) Any of these, at any moment, can send my heart pounding and my hands shaking uncontrollably. At other times, nothing happens. I just never know.

I carried on teaching school to my children after September 11. It wasn't until after we buried my father that it all came crashing in on me. The numbness had worn off. The pain of burying my father so long after his death was intense. I began to ask questions. I could face God then. So after we returned home from Virginia, fresh from my father's graveside, the kids and I spent a couple of months off, and I searched for answers, answers about 9/11, answers about homeschooling, answers about God. Everything had to change. The way I thought about my family, the way I perceived God, the way I prayed, even the way I taught my children. It all had to change in order to find a place where I could live within my grief.

Recently, I saw an advertisement for an upcoming television special about the children of 9/11. I thought to myself, *I feel so bad for them.* Then I realized that *I* am a child of 9/11. I may have been an adult already, but I lost my father that day also. Still, it must be worse for a young child to lose his or her parent. I am thankful that I had the opportunity to have my father for as long as I did. At least I was an adult before I lost him. Yet, I still lost my daddy, and the wound runs deep.

I am wounded. I feel wounded. I try to go about my life as though everything is fine, like I am okay, but I have been lacerated to my core, and I carry the hurt with me always. At times, it reopens and festers, then it begins to heal, but I will never be wholly cured. I will carry it with me forever. However, that does not mean that I won't endure, that I won't carry on. To live my life is what my father would have wanted. He never wished to be an imposition on anyone. He never wanted to make a fuss. I often wonder what he would think of all the attention he has gotten since September 11.

My husband and I decided to have a night out. We settled on a movie. As we entered the theater, we had the good fortune to run into a couple who lived in our neighborhood. We had a pleasant conversation, and then went to our seats as the previews to upcoming movies appeared on the screen. I settled down in my place. Suddenly the sound of jet engines came over the speakers and a view of New York City shone on the screen. I shuddered. My heart began to pound as the engines grew louder. I shut my eyes. Tears squeezed out from under my lids. Trembling, I let out an audible sigh. My husband grabbed my hand and held it tight. I wanted to stand up and scream, to run from the theater. But I just sat there and endured the moment. The movie previewed was *World Trade Center* with Nicholas Cage. Five years it had been and still my reaction was of trauma. I cannot get away from it. After the movie, my neighbor came over to me and said, "All I could do was think of you. Here you and your husband came to the movies to get away from it all, and this is what you have to see."

My grief is always before me, for this event was a public tragedy. We all share a part of it. We all have to grieve it. So it is always before my face, year after year. Every anniversary, as people honor those lost on September 11, the wound is ripped open anew. Yet, if everyone forgot, that would be painful also. I do not want them to forget. I want everyone to remember what happened that day. I want everyone to remember our loved ones lost.

My father's death wasn't an accident or an illness, somebody did this to him, and that makes it so much worse. My father had not done anything worthy of such hate, yet hatred killed him. He did not deserve to die in this manner. He was a gentle man, who should have lived to an old age then peacefully slip from this world into the next. Yet wishing it does not make it so.

Many that live deserve death. And some that die deserve life. Can you give it to them? Then do not be too eager to deal out death in judgement. For even the very wise cannot see all ends.

~ J. R. R. Tolkien[2]

*Even the very wise cannot see all ends…* That thought resonates within me. We don't know what the result of September 11 will be down through the ages. May it be that there is a greater plan than the pain we feel right now? Some greater good that will benefit some better cause upon this world?

> Hear ye not the hum
> Of mighty workings?
> ~John Keats[3]

There are no simple answers. You can't just say, "It was God's will." That thought will not float anymore. It is patronizing and it answers nothing. Acceptance is easier if we understand why. But really, what answer could God give that would justify in our eyes the death of our loved ones.

> Oft hope is born,
> when all is forlorn.
> ~ J. R. R. Tolkien[4]

There is no answer good enough that we could understand to cancel the loss we feel. Yet, often we find hope when it seems that there is nothing left to cling to.

Man's inhumanity against man. Our innocence was shattered that day. An experience like that changes you. The entire world has been altered in some way by the events of September 11. Evil is a force not caused by anything else. This Evil is not new. We have seen it throughout time. We have seen the face of Evil before in the nefarious acts that man has committed against his fellow man. We saw it in Nero, in Diocletian, in Hitler. This was the first time Evil of this magnitude had been seen on American soil, and we experienced it firsthand.

Nero, who ruled the Roman Empire from 54 to 68 AD, is credited by Tertullian (c. 155-230) as the first persecutor of Christians.[5] Many believe it was under the rule of Nero that the Apostles Peter and Paul were executed.[6] Stories are told of countless accounts of cruelty and torture at the hands of his administration. After the Great Fire that swept through Rome, Nero placed the blame on the new religious sect known as Christianity. Many Christians were arrested and crucified. Many others were fed to the wild beasts in the Circus Maximus or burned at the stake serving as human candles in Nero's garden.[7]

Diocletian ruled the Roman Empire from 284 to 305 AD. Feeling threatened by the unwillingness of Christians to follow his edict to return to the traditional pagan religion of Rome, Diocletian aggressively attempted to enforce his laws by participating in the extreme cruelty of unspeakable tortures and executions of countless Christians. This constituted the Roman Empire's last, largest, and bloodiest official persecution of the Christian church. Yet, all the bloodshed and suffering did not bring the results Diocletian intended. The willingness of the many suffering martyrs to surrender their lives for their faith only strengthened the resolve of their fellow Christians. In fact, within twenty-five years of these persecutions, the Christian religion became the empire's national faith under the Emperor Constantine.[8]

All remember the atrocities performed under the authority of Hitler, the annihilation of so many innocent people. The only reason was pure hatred for what was different. Atrocities unnumbered, his New Order condemned an estimated seventeen million to unspeakable acts of inhumanity. One cannot comprehend how any human being could ever perpetrate so much evil.

Then came the shocking cold bloodedness of September 11. It was the face of Evil we saw that day. Do we let Evil rule that day? Evil certainly caused the day. But do we surrender to that Evil? Or do we lift ourselves beyond the ashes to new life? What happened was definitely bad. Can good come out of it? Evil caused the day, but Love ruled it. I saw Love in the eyes of those who watched in horror as the events unfolded; compassion shone on every face. I saw Love in the unity of the American people. I saw Love in every gift given to the families from the American people, in the teddy bears and homemade cards schoolchildren gave to my children. I saw Love in the memorial quilt sewn for me in memory of my father. I saw Love in the hearts of those strangers who held hands at the moment of their death. I saw Love as the people evacuated Manhattan Island in an orderly and calm fashion. I saw Love as those firefighters and police officers entered the burning buildings to help all they could, and I saw the Love they had as they laid down their lives for a stranger. Evil may have caused the day, but Love ruled it.

> Now, we have inscribed a new memory alongside those others. It's a memory of tragedy and shock, of loss and mourning. But not only of loss and mourning. It's also a memory of bravery and self-sacrifice, and the love that lays down its life for a friend—even a friend whose name it never knew.
>
> ~ President George W. Bush[9]

> The eyes of the LORD
> are on the righteous,
> And His ears are open
> to their cry.
> The face of the LORD is
> against those who do evil,
> To cut off the
> remembrance of them
> from the earth.
>
> ~Psalm 34:15-16

Now, ten years later, do we return to life as it was? Or do we cling to these lessons of Love shown us that day as we face difficult times ahead. Do we ignore the suffering of our neighbors, or do we take the time to care for them? Do we let Love rule our lives? We can make September 11 a day of hate or we can make it a day of love as we look to the kindness and compassion of the American people, of the world, of the victims as they faced death so bravely.

The Lord, He never rests, nor does He ever slumber. In His sleepless vigilance, God is always watchful. He will not allow our foot to slip, but preserves us so that we can hold fast. (Psalms 121: 1-3) The foundation of Christ upon which we stand does not move. Nero is gone, Diocletian is gone, Hitler is gone, even Bin Laden is gone, but righteousness lives on. They could not destroy it; they could not silence it. Love endures. They have no hold over us if we do not let them.

# Episode 9

# NOT ALONE

*Blessed are those who mourn,*
*For they shall be comforted.*

*~Matthew 5:4*

It is a lonely feeling, standing apart as a solitary figure entombed in the dismal shroud of anguish. No one around you can understand how you feel, why the pain is still so bad. At times, they grow impatient with the sorrow that surrounds you. Even though they may be too polite to say what is on their mind, their actions seem to say, "Why can't you just get over it and move on?" or "What you need to do is put it all behind you."

*Get over it.* I wish I knew how. Maybe it is not that we are to get over it, or even put it behind us. Maybe it is how we rise above it that matters; to feel the loss and accept the pain, incorporating it into our lives so completely that it becomes a part of us from which we draw strength. Can our own suffering really strengthen us? Is it possible to rise above the pain to something greater? Though I feel alone, am I really alone in my sorrow?

"The eyes of the LORD are on the righteous, and His ears are open to their cry." (Psalm 34:15) The Lord hears our cry and lifts us out of our afflictions. He did not promise that there would be no troubles, that there would be no broken hearts. In fact, He promised just the opposite. John 16:33 says that in this world we *will* have tribulation. It is a promise. However we are not to despair, but be encouraged, for Christ reminds us that He has overcome the world. There is nothing too difficult for Him; even death cannot stand against His mighty power. So be emboldened and have peace within the midst of suffering.

In this world, we will have pain and sorrow. We are not called to live a happy, carefree life. We are charged to participate in His sacrifice. Jesus summons us to "take up the cross" and follow Him. (Mark 10:21)

> *For to you it has been granted on behalf of Christ, not only to believe in Him, but also to suffer for His sake.*
> ~ Philippians 1:29

Peter states, "It is better, if it is the will of God, to suffer for doing good than for doing evil." (1 Peter 3:17) For what credit is there to suffer for our own faults? But when we are good and right and yet suffer for the cause of Christ, then as we take it patiently, we are to be commended. It is for this we are called, because "Christ also suffered for us." In doing so, He has left an example for us to follow. (Peter 2:19-21)

It is said that God often deems it necessary that his people should suffer. According to the American theologian Albert Barnes (1798-1870), "There are effects to be accomplished by affliction which can be secured in no other way; and some of the happiest results on the soul of a Christian, some of the brightest traits of character, are the effect of trials."[1]

This being for the purpose that even as we do good, yet spoken against, we may prove ourselves a true Christian. If all things are ordered by the will of God, then this includes even our own sufferings. But we know that God does not tempt anyone (James

1:13), and nothing evil comes from God (1 Tim. 4:4), then why do we suffer?

Matthew Henry (1662-1714), the English commentator on the Bible, states, "The example of Christ is an argument for patience under sufferings." For Christ, who knew no sin, suffered for those who knew no righteousness in order that those unworthy could be reconciled to God and to bring them to eternal glory. "If Christ could not be freed from sufferings, why should Christians think to be so?"[2]

If this is true, why then would anyone want to be a Christian? Why be a child of God, unless it is for some Hope. For there must be a Hope or we will not walk forward, but lie down and give up. What keeps us going? Our Hope is this, that being children of God, then we are "heirs of God and joint heirs with Christ, if indeed we suffer with Him, that we may also be glorified together." (Romans 8:17) We have this promise that

> Brethren, I do not count myself to have apprehended; but one thing I do, forgetting those things which are behind and reaching forward to those things which are ahead, I press toward the goal for the prize of the upward call of God in Christ Jesus.
> - Philippians 3:13-14

we will partake in the same eternal glory as Christ, receiving our portion of God Himself. Yet, suffering lies in the path to Glory, and we must endure if we are to reach our inheritance. If we allow suffering to discourage us so that we turn off the path, then our reward will not be achieved. However, if we endure to the end, if we continue through the trials and tribulations of this world, glory will be our end, the end of suffering for all time. Therefore, press on to the mark with your eyes fixed on Jesus, never taking your eyes off the goal set before you.

We are to forget those things which are behind, for who can put their hand to the plow while looking over their shoulder? (Luke 9:62) We cannot spend our lives dwelling on past hurts. If we do, our furrows will be crooked. One who plows a field must look forward, for as he moves ahead, if he looks behind, his rows will not be straight. We are all called to suffer in this world. We cannot constantly look back with regret as we count the cost. To be effective, we must trod ever forward. One could say that to follow Christ is to give everything or nothing. "Then He said to them all, 'If anyone desires to come after Me, let him deny himself, and take up his cross daily, and follow Me.'" (Luke 9:23) He did not say lay down your burden and follow me unhindered by the trials of life. He said, "*take up your cross* and follow me." Our cross we must carry.

> *Come to Me, all you who labor and are heavy laden, and I will give you rest. Take My yoke upon you and learn from Me, for I am gentle and lowly in heart, and you will find rest for your souls. For My yoke is easy and My burden is light.*
> – Matthew 11: 28-30

In a radio interview marking the ten-year anniversary of 9/11, my brother made this statement: "Life is sort of a preparation for disaster. Sorrow is going to come in one form or another. To think it won't is naive. And so, the way we live our life is investing in how we are going to deal with that sorrow when it comes."[3] And when it comes, for we know it will, we do not want to be unprepared or to suffer unaided.

*His yoke is easy, His burden is light.* A yoke is a wooden beam that binds two animals together, so that together, they can pull a load. The words *subjugate* and *servitude* are related to the word *yoke*. So then, to be yoked is to be placed under subjugation to something or someone while being bound to another. Christ did not say take off your yoke and walk away. He invites us to trade the heavy yoke of the world and to place His yoke upon ourselves. It is His yoke. We share the yoke with Him. He is there with us as we carry this yoke. He is yoked to us. He is there to give us His hand so that He can rescue us. So be strong and have good courage. You have nothing to fear, for the Lord your God goes with you. "He will not leave you nor forsake you." (Deuteronomy 31:6)

I am determined to struggle through to the other side. Many have offered me advice on how to deal with my grief and the trauma of September 11. I am often told that I have to let it go. I realize people just want to help me. It is uncomfortable for them to see me struggle, but I must go through the process. I cannot just skip over the elements of grief and be done. I have to wade through the muck

> But these evils can be amended, so strong and gay a spirit is in him. His grief he will not forget; but it will not darken his heart, it will teach him wisdom.
> - J. R. R. Tolkien[4]

and mire of it until I get to the other side. No one can fix it. No pill can relieve it. But I am not alone. I have a Savior who wades in with me and holds my hand. He does not build a bridge over the pain to free us of our suffering, for what do we gain in that. But He enters the struggle with us, supports us, and guides us to the far shore.

> You number my wanderings; Put my tears into Your bottle; Are they not in Your book?
> - Psalm 56:8

Edwin Hubbell Chapin wrote that "out of suffering have emerged the strongest souls; the most massive characters are seared with scars; martyrs have put on their coronation robes glittering with fire, and through their tears have the sorrowful first seen the gates of Heaven."[5]

I have shed many tears; God has kept a record of them. He did not let my tears fall to the ground to be forgotten. The Lord has collected them and placed them in a bottle, to preserve them as a memorial to my sorrow, a lachrymatory of my grief. He keeps them close, for each tear is precious to Him. He will never forget that they were shed.

It is not wrong to weep, to pour out our sorrow in tears. The psalmist David cried. Jesus wept. (John 11:35) Christ mourned for the loss of His good friend. He wept for the grief Mary and Martha felt for their dead brother. Jesus wept, even though He knew He was about to raise Lazarus from the dead. This is not a God who

> *The righteous cry out, and the LORD hears,*
> *And delivers them out of all their troubles.*
> *The LORD is near to those who have a broken heart,*
> *And saves such as have a contrite spirit.*
> *~ Psalm 34:17-18*

has no compassion, who passes judgment on creation without mercy. This is a God who weeps for our sorrows.

Shadrach, Meshach, and Abednego, the story does not end with the furnace. But I think the key is in the word *through*, for we do go *through*, we do not stay *in* the furnace. There is an end to our trouble if we stand firm. The fire had no power. For even as the three young men stood within the flames of the furnace, they were not alone, but a fourth stood beside them. They were delivered from the fire, their clothes were not singed, and there was not even the smell of smoke upon them. We are not alone. The Lord is not a God who hovers on the outside. He steps into the furnace with us. And so I say "even so" I will serve the Lord.

My father believed this. He used to sing the song "Through It All" in church. The song speaks to the fact that no matter what happens in life, through the strife and disappointments, through the sorrows and agitations, God is there to see us through. That "in every situation, God gave me blessed consolation, that my trials come to only make me strong."[6] The words speak my father's testimony. How can I do any less?

So then, I am learning to lean on God, even when I do not understand. As the Children of Israel wandered in the desert, so too do we wander in this world, searching for the Promised Land. Although God had sent them into the wilderness, yet he said, "You don't have to go it alone. I will show you the way, all you need do is follow Me." And so as a pillar of cloud and a pillar of fire, the Lord led the Israelites out of the wild and into their rest. He was with them always, providing for all their needs, guiding them through the empty wasteland. So too, He promised us that He would be with us.

> And I heard a loud voice from heaven saying,
> "Behold, the tabernacle of God is with men, and He will dwell with them, and they shall be His people. God Himself will be with them and be their God."
> - Revelation 21:3

How beautiful it is to behold the torn veil, for we have direct access to the Father. Nothing or no one can deny us admittance before God. As we walk through the Holy of Holies, the Shekinah, the glorious presence of God, shines out upon us. The warmth of His proximity radiates upon my face. As His rays of power and light reach out to me in dark places, I hear Him say, "I will never leave you nor forsake you."

So what then can man do to me? For the keeper of my soul watches me. Though God's protection is not always for our bodies, it is a constant for our souls. And in the end, it is our final home that is most important. This mortal coil which we cling to so ardently is not what *it* is all about. This world is not my home. I am just passing through it on my journey home. In 1 Peter 2:11, the apostle calls us

> So we may boldly say:
> "The LORD is my helper;
> I will not fear.
> What can man do to me?"
> - Hebrews 13:5-6

sojourners and pilgrims, strangers in the world, passing on to our eternal home, seeking a heavenly country. "You sojourn in the body; you are pilgrims in this world."[7] This land we seek is a better country, where the Father's house is located, "for our citizenship is in heaven." (Philippians 3:20) While we journey, we face many hardships upon the road. Thieves wait to ambush us, the weather of this world becomes harsh, and so as we travel we grow weary. But looking to the goal, we must endure if we desire to reach our homeland, a land where we will never have to labor again, and we will have rest from our journey.

For all that is in the world, all the evil that men do, all the selfish pride inflicted upon the innocent, is not of the Lord, but is of this world. Yet, do not be discouraged, the world is passing away, and the evil it holds will cease to be. But those who love the Lord and do the will of the Father will abide with Him forever. (1 John 2:16-17) Many in the past have lived by faith, and yet returned home to glory before the Promises were fulfilled. They trusted in God, having seen the assurance of them from far off. They lived them, embraced them, confessing that they were strangers on the earth. (Hebrews 11:13)

As sojourners with Christ, we are called not to rest while we are here, but to suffer, because Christ also suffered for us, leaving us a perfect example to follow in His steps. Why do the innocent suffer? Why did Christ suffer? Christ "committed no sin, nor was deceit found in His mouth," yet he suffered so that we have a rescue from this foreign land. (1 Peter 2:22) If we follow in His footsteps, we will find our way along the difficult road. He does not take us

> *Hear my prayer, O LORD,*
> *And give ear to my cry;*
> *Do not be silent at my tears;*
> *For I am a stranger with You,*
> *A sojourner,*
> *as all my fathers were.*
> — Psalm 39:12

off the road. We still have to travel the hard miles, but He has provided a guide for us so that we can see the way.

For Christ when He was reviled, He did not retaliate. When He suffered, He did not threaten, but committed Himself to His righteous judge. He bore our sins upon His person, carried alone the weight of all humanity's condemnation, and bore it all upon the cross, so that we, who deserve death, might live for righteousness. It is by His "stripes you were healed. For you were like sheep going astray, but have now returned to the Shepherd and Overseer of your souls." (1 Peter 2:23-25)

> *For the time has come for judgment to begin at the house of God; and if it begins with us first, what will be the end of those who do not obey the gospel of God? Now...*
> *If the righteous one is scarcely saved,*
> *Where will the ungodly and the sinner appear?*
> — 1 Peter 4:17-18

Do not think it strange that we suffer painful trials in this world. We are admonished to rejoice to the extent that we are sharing in the suffering of the Christ, that when His glory is revealed, we may also be *glad with exceeding joy*. This does not mean that we are to be happy when trials and loss come our way, but we are to think of our final goal of glory and rejoice that we are able to share with Christ the inheritance of heaven. Though we suffer for a time, we will rejoice with Christ forevermore. So if for a time you are impeached for the sake of Christ, do not be dismayed, for the Spirit of God rests upon you. Though some may not understand, to you His Glory will be evident. So don't suffer for evil doing, but suffer for the cause of Christ. If anyone endures pain as one belonging to Christ, let him not be ashamed, but glorify God in His trials. (1 Peter 4:12-16)

"Therefore let those who suffer according to the will of God commit their souls *to Him* in doing good, as to a faithful Creator." (1 Peter 4:19) God will not relax His hold on me, He will not let go. Yet, who am I that God is mindful of me? (Psalm 8) God is so much bigger than even the universe, yet He looks upon me with concern. How is it that this great God even notices me or is concerned with the sorrows that come my way? Yet the very hairs upon my head are numbered. I do not even know myself that well. So careful is the Providence of God that not even one hair can fall from my head without the Lord taking notice. If God were willing to lay the sins of all the world, past, present, and future, upon the shoulders of His Son, if God were willing to condemn His own Son to suffer the penalty of death for those sins so that we would not have to, how then would He leave us to suffer this world without His concern? For we are more valuable than a sparrow, yet one of these little common birds cannot fall apart from the will of the Father, for He remembers each one of them. (Luke 12:7)

We look to meaning in the world of flesh, but God looks to the spirit. Our healing is spiritual. At times, it is our body that God heals, but His big concern is for our soul. For what profit is there if we save our earthly body and lose our very soul? For what then can be exchanged for our soul? (Matthew 16:26) Our concern is now and our present discomfort. God's concern is for eternity. We want happiness and peace now. God wants us to share in His glory for evermore. The fires of life purify us. We are tempered in the flames of adversity. As a parent sees the future for their child, so God sees the future for His own. A child does not see the benefit to proper study, yet the teacher knows the future and encourages the student to work hard to build a better tomorrow. The student is forced to suffer the trials of hard work and difficult lessons so that his future prospect

> Who knows your
> disappointments
> Who hears each time you cry
> Who understands your
> heartaches
> Who dries the tears
> from your eyes?
> ~ W. F. Lakey and V. B. Ellis [8]

will provide him comfort in a well-bestowed career. Does then the parent or the teacher not love the child? They allow him to suffer through the struggles of learning. Has the teacher or the parent deserted the child? Of course not, they are simply looking out for the welfare of the child, being unkind to be kind. Even though the child is made to suffer, the parent and teacher are there to help the child along the way. Even so, we have a Savior who is there for us.

Have you heard? He loves you.

# Episode 10

# GOD'S SOVEREIGNTY

*But the LORD is in His holy temple.*
*Let all the earth keep silence before Him.*
*~ Habakkuk 2:20*

As evening descended over the Sea of Galilee, the sky rosy red as the setting sun painted the gathering clouds, Jesus and his disciples set off across the lake in little boats desiring to get to the other side. Tired from teaching the multitudes that pressed toward Him, Jesus lay down within the stern of the boat and quickly fell asleep upon a pillow. On a sudden, a great windstorm arose. The waves beat down upon the little boats until they began to fill with water, threatening to sink with all on board. The disciples trembled as they bailed out the water and pulled in the sails. All the while, their Master slept upon the pillow. Finally, when their fear overcame them and they could not take it anymore, they went to Jesus and awoke Him saying, "Teacher, do You not care that we are perishing? How is it that You sleep while we suffer to save our lives?"

Calmly, Jesus rose to His feet and stood, facing the storm. Raising His hand against the winds and the waves, Jesus called out to the sea, "Peace, be still!" And the wind and the waves ceased, and a great calm fell over the water. The men sighed in relief and looked upon one another in disbelief. All thought, "Why did we need to struggle for so long, when all the while our Master could have helped us? Why did He not prevent the storm in the first place?"

Jesus knew their thoughts and sighed to Himself as He looked at the men with love in His eyes. Then He spoke to them, saying, "Why are you so fearful? Did you think that I would not help you? How is it that you have no faith?" Then Jesus returned to the stern, lay down upon His pillow, and went to sleep. Looking with fear upon their Master, the disciples stood in awe. Speaking to one another they said, "Who can this be, that even the wind and the sea obey Him!" (Mark 4:35-41)

What then, do we murmur against God as though we know better than He who stretched out the very foundation of the universe? How little is our understanding? How presumptuous is our condemnation? Christ asks, "Why are you so fearful? How is it that you have no faith?" When calamity strikes, humanity always questions God. I am no different. Immediately we demand answers. But who are we to demand anything of God, yet it is in our very nature to need answers. It is what makes us uniquely human.

God allows us a time to respond to circumstances in our humanity. He patiently waits while we carry on without understanding. God allowed Job to question Him for a long time. Is it okay to question God, to seek out the answers to those tough questions? He knows our thoughts anyway. We might as well voice them. I voiced my complaint to God often, questioning Him regarding the involvement of my family in the events of September 11. He patiently listened to me rant, as I sought for understanding. But a time comes when He says, "Enough!" and God answers.

He reminds us that He is God; all sovereignty belongs to Him. Through our trials, God wants us to speak without doubt of the moral rightness and mercy of His government to inspire confidence in the goodness of God. To throw doubt upon the councils of the Lord is to breed disbelief in the world concerning the Lord. This is counterproductive to the will of God, whose sole purpose is to save the lost. We presume much when we speak as though we have understanding regarding the ways of God.

> Then the LORD answered
> Job out of the whirlwind,
> and said:
> "Who is this who darkens
> counsel
> By words without
> knowledge …
> Where were you when I laid
> the foundations of the earth?
> Tell Me, if you have
> understanding. …
> Or who laid its cornerstone,
> When the morning stars
> sang together?"
> ~ Job 38:1-2, 4, 6-7

The Lord calls on Job to compare God to Job's own being. God is immortal, Job is mortal; God is all-knowing, Job has limited understanding; God is all-powerful, Job lives in weakness. "Our darkening the counsels of God's wisdom with our folly, is a great provocation to God. Humble faith and sincere obedience see farthest and best into the will of the Lord." (Matthew Henry[1])

While visiting my mother sometime after September 11, as we were all struggling with our own feelings of loss and betrayal, my mother called to me. I went downstairs to see what the matter was. She told me something strange had happened. She had been reading a pamphlet about grief and loss that the Pentagon had given to the victims' families when she came across a statement

> *Shall the one who contends with the Almighty correct Him? He who rebukes God, let him answer it.*
> ~ Job 40:2

that shook her. The words, "Do not question the ways of God" appeared on a page in boldface type. The words seemed to rise above the other letters upon the page. We searched the pamphlet but could never find the words again. They weren't there.

Job responds by saying he will cover his mouth and keep quiet. "Though I have spoken, now I will listen." (Job 40:4-5) The Lord instructs Job to present his case as before a judge to prove that he fully comprehends before he condemns God. Job has opened the topic, now he must finish it. "Prepare yourself to make an answer and declare to Me your wisdom, for can you govern the universe, can you annul My judgment, do you have the arm of God?" To complain against God is to say that He has dealt wrongly, that we know better than God does what is best. Only the Lord has the wisdom to know how and when to govern. It is not for us to instruct God, but He is to teach us. We cannot even rescue our own souls from His justice, but we must commit ourselves into His hands to save us by His Grace. Therefore, who are we to tell God what is just and fair. (Job 40:7-14)

God goes into a long discourse of His power, reminding Job who He is. In the book of Job, chapters 38-39 delve into great detail of all the works the Lord has done with His mighty hands, reminding us that He is sovereign. God has complete authority in all times. God's power is overwhelming. We must be careful not to forget to whom we speak. The Lord is our King and His very Being demands our respect. God knows

> *I have heard of You by the hearing of the ear, But now my eye sees You.*
> ~ Job 42:5

our thoughts, our hurts, our questions, but we must be cautious of our tone. Question God in order to gain understanding, but do not question His authority, for by His act of creation He owns us, having the right to direct our lives. We are not more righteous than God. The Lord can do everything and no purpose of His can be withheld from His will. The counsels of God are too wonderful to behold, and we often utter without understanding. We speak so often that I wonder if we cannot hear God for all our complaining.

Job is satisfied. He has seen God for who He is. He has a clear understanding of the Shekinah, the glory of the Lord. He rests in the knowledge of the supreme justice of God, placing his trust in the Lord's judgment.

Do we see God in the workings of the world? With enlightened spirit we can see God for who He is, surpassing the understanding of what we thought we knew. Beyond the dark veil of this world, we can see the presence of God, the very face of Yahweh watching and directing events from the very foundation of this world to our present time, the laying down with perfect precision the commission of time for the fulfillment of His creation.

> His glory covered the heavens,
> And the earth was full of His praise.
> His brightness was like the light;
> He had rays flashing from His hand,
> And there His power was hidden.
>
> ~ Habakkuk 3: 3-4

Yet, how can a just God allow the destruction of innocent people at the hands of evil men? I heard someone say that in the events of September 11, we were burned by religion and he wants no part of it. One cannot separate the events of September 11 from the role of religion in this world. It is inherently a religious battle between fanatical

Islam and the Judeo-Christian ideology of this country. That in the name of religion, many terrors have plagued this world cannot be questioned. Men of all religions have done terrible things in the name of God. We may have been burned by religion, but religion is a man-made institution. God is not about religion, He is about Love. What men chose to do in the name of God does not make it of God. We are not fools to believe in God. We are fools to follow blindly an ideology of hate and intolerance.

When the news came that Bin Laden had been killed, people ran into the streets cheering and celebrating, reveling in justice and in the resolution of revenge. I only felt a profound sadness, a sadness that followed

> At the fall of man the beauty of the Earth was marred, the evil of the Enemy "and the blight of his hatred flowed out thence... and dyed the earth with blood."
> ~ J. R. R. Tolkien[2]

me for days. I was glad the man could do no more harm to this world, yet it really changed nothing. His death did not bring back my father. Another will rise up to take Bin Laden's place. This act did not end Evil.

Yet, who can know the mind of God? Man has no understanding of the purposes of God, striving always with His Power, being at variance with His Will instead of loving Him and allowing Him to guide them. God created man with free will, but this gift comes with a price. Man often uses his free will to choose evil. As long as we live upon this earth, the free will of man will touch our lives for good or for ill.

So the prophet Habakkuk cried out to God as he watched his city encircled by the enemy, "How long will I cry out to You and You will not hear? How long until You save us?" (Habakkuk 1:2) At times, we even cry out, "Are You even there, God? Why do You not answer me? I do not understand what is happening. Won't You answer me?"

Then God spoke, replying to the prophet's question, "Look among the nations and watch—Be utterly astounded! For I will work a work in your days which you would not believe, though it were told you." (Habakkuk 1:5)

So I wait and watch. Soon I shall see.

# Episode 11

# ALL IN HIS HANDS

*My Father's way may twist and turn,*
*My heart may throb and ache,*
*But in my soul I'm glad I know,*
*He maketh no mistake.*

*~A. M. Overton[1]*

The Spirit moves, God does not leave us alone. Our heart stirs, but we do not understand. As Jacob did, so we too wrestle with God and our hip is put out of joint. (Genesis 32:22-32) If everything that happened to us were good, what example would we be to a suffering world? How could we relate to the common man? We all share in the sorrow of this world, of the products of Free Will. We should stand out as a beacon of hope, for we do have a Hope. Though all our plans fail and all our hopes fade, we can place our trust in Christ, for the Hope He brings us is a different kind of hope. It is a Hope based on the goodness and truth of God that does not disappoint. The flame of power we receive through the love of God is quickened in the heart by the infusing of the Holy Spirit that enlightens the soul with the peace that comes from our Hope in the Lord. (Romans 5:5) What seems to us to make no sense may one day appear as clear as glass, as we look past the trial toward the goal. There is still so much I cannot see, yet still I hold on and trust to Hope.

Joseph had a dream of his greatness, which bred jealousy in his brothers. Sold as a slave, Joseph suffered fear and humiliation. Accused of crimes he did not commit, he was cast into prison for twenty years. Through it all, Joseph trusted God to set things right. Lifted up to the position of second in command of the nation of Egypt, Joseph became the instrument of salvation for his people. As he confronted his brothers who had been the cause of all his suffering, Joseph spoke, "But as for you, you meant evil against me; but God meant it for good." (Genesis 50:20) God leaves the sinner wholly to his own will, but out of the issue of chaos and calamity that follows, God works it out to bring forth good. Can good come out of this tragedy as a phoenix rises from the ashes to new life? Only time and eternity will tell.

> Fair shall the end be...
> though long and hard
> shall be the road.
> ~ J. R. R. Tolkien[2]

Would I have told my father's story if he had not died as he did? I don't think so. Now his testimony, his voice is heard sounding down through the ages. How great will his influence be? Is this the reason, then, that he died? I cannot answer that. But certainly as I sit here, it is a Good that has risen out of something terrible.

Other positives have arisen out of this tragedy. I have returned to doing things I once loved. I read more for pleasure. The loss of my father has motivated me to pursue writing, a passion I have longed for since I was thirteen, but never had the courage to undertake. I have decided that if I am to get anything done it is now or never, for we never know how much time we have.

Sometimes the path is difficult, and we grow weary and we wish we did not have to face what lies ahead. No one can know our hurts and our sorrows. Yet the Lord knows, for He has walked this path before us. All we must do is follow Him. Though that path may be slick and we may stumble, the Lord has gone before us and marked the way.

There is a comfort even in tragedy if one walks according to God's will. "For the steps of a good man are ordered by the Lord" (Psalm 37:23), therefore each step

> Oh, the cross has wondrous glory!
> Oft I've proved this to be true,
> When I'm in the way so narrow,
> I can see a pathway through;
> And how sweetly Jesus whispers,
> "Take the cross, thou
> need'st not fear,
> For I've tried the way
> before thee,
> And the glory lingers near."
> - William Hunter[3]

taken must pass before the sanction of God. With the Lord's ultimate control, the fabric of His plan is woven, each of His children being a single thread. It is a strange comfort to know that nothing can befall you without God's approval. "And we know that all things work together for good to those who love God, to those who are the called according to *His* purpose." (Romans 8:28) This is not to say that all things are *good*, but that they *work to the good* of our future, to fulfill the ultimate good of God's plan, a plan of redemption for humanity.

There is no question in my mind that on the morning of September 11 my dear father followed God and entered into his glory. It *is* a strange comfort to know that even in death, he was walking in God's will. I need to believe this. I have to trust in the Lord's judgments or else my faith will be shaken. It could not all have been for nothing, for no reason. That would be too hard to bear. I must simply be still, to be silent and wait, and know that He is God. (Psalm 46:10) I must live by faith.

After September 11, we were on our way to church. While

sitting at a red light, we witnessed an accident. A car ran the light and crashed into another in the intersection. The sound was terrible. One of the cars caught fire. The other spun out of control as it headed straight for us. I yelled, "Not us!" as I put my hand out to brace myself. What happened next was amazing. As the car sped toward us, it suddenly stopped without slowing down just

> *The steps of a good man are ordered by the LORD, And He delights in his way. Though he fall, he shall not be utterly cast down; For the LORD upholds him with His hand.*
> ~ Psalm 37:23-24

inches from our car. It was as if an invisible hand reached out and restrained the car just in time. We all sat amazed, looking at one another. The driver in the other car looked at us with a stunned look on his face. We all knew a miracle had happened.

> *Trust in the LORD with all your heart, And lean not on your own understanding; In all your ways acknowledge Him, And He shall direct your paths.*
> ~ Proverbs 3:5-6

So then how do we rectify in our minds, in our souls, when at times God's protection is upon us and not on someone else. Was God showing me that day that He is still in control? That He still has power to intervene in my life?

My father trusted God. His path was directed by the Lord. Therefore, I have to trust that his steps were indeed ordered by the Lord. Many believe that tribulations come as a result of our disobedience, that God's protection for our body is removed when we are off the path. This is the reasoning given to Job in his sufferings by his well-meaning friends.

Sometimes trials do happen because of our disobedience, to bring us around and heal our relationship with God. However this does not answer all the reasons. Sometimes it is just not anything we have or have not done, but maybe it is for what we will do with it, what we will make of it. We have to trust that God's judgments are just and merciful for the greater good. I do not know if this answers anything, but it helps to think that the sacrifice of my loved one was not without reason, that it may serve a greater purpose, though I may not see it yet. Behind it something greater is working.

In Tolkien's trilogy, *The Lord of the Rings*, the wise, old wizard Gandalf speaks words of comfort to Frodo, the young hobbit who has taken on the responsibility of saving their world from the evil plans of the enemy, known as Sauron the Ring-maker. As I watched Gandalf speak these words upon the screen, I was moved by the thought that events are often more than they appear.

> Behind that there was something else at work, beyond any design of the Ring-maker. I can put it no plainer than by saying that Bilbo was meant to find the Ring, and not by its maker. In which case you also were meant to have it. And that may be an encouraging thought.
>
> ~J. R. R. Tolkien[4]

*For now we see in a mirror, dimly, but then face to face. Now I know in part, but then I shall know just as I also am known.*

*~ 1 Corinthians 13:12*

Tolkien used this scene to explain his thoughts regarding Providence. I have found this a very encouraging passage. If we replace "Ring-maker" with the words "Evil" or "Satan," and the role of the "Ring" with the bad that happens in our lives, I think we can see clearly what Tolkien was attempting to relay to the reader. God is in control. These things were meant to happen. We cannot see all ends, but it is strangely comforting to know God directs events in our lives. That is not to say God caused the bad in our lives to happen, but He certainly can turn that evil into the fulfillment of His original purpose. He has a plan that when acted upon by outside forces, as a result of the gift of free will, which takes the path outside of His design, He will use the results in a way that best completes the original plan. God takes the intent of evil's objective out of Satan's hands and works beyond the plan of evil against our lives, creating a new purpose, bent to His own design. No matter what we do as men of free will, God will work it out according to His will. What we see as bad may prove to be for a good purpose. Our eyes are limited to the here and now. God's eyes are eternal.

We think in fleshly terms, we are programmed that way. But God thinks in the Spirit and all He does is for the purpose of spiritual substances, matter beyond the scope of our limited human minds. For now, I see in part, then I will have understanding, the full understanding of the plans of God. The Lord alone knows the things of God, for its depth is unfathomable by mortals. While man can search out and discover the works of nature, he can by no means understand the workings of

> But where can wisdom
> be found?
> And where is the place of
> understanding?
> Man does not know its
> value,
> Nor is it found in the
> land of the living.
> From where then does
> wisdom come?
> And where is the place of
> understanding?
> It is hidden from the eyes
> of all living.
> - Job 28:12-13, 20-21

the spirit except by special revelation from God. All the universe that stretches beyond comprehension is still a limited space to God's understanding. As such, our ability to attain understanding of the works of God is limited to this world at hand, constricted and bound to this present universe. Unattainable, the knowledge of God is too high a thing for man to apprehend.

Understanding is a *twofold wisdom*. There is a wisdom that is hidden from man, though we may seek it, it is not revealed to us for it does not belong to us. Yet there is a wisdom that God allows us to fathom, one that belongs to His children, which when studied and looked upon provides us with a glimpse of this God who is a mystery.[5]

> One day's events, and one man's affairs, have such reference to, and so hang one upon another, that He only, to whom all is open, and who sees the whole at one view, can rightly judge of every part.
>
> – Mathew Henry[6]

Each event builds upon the next in such an intricate fashion that we cannot see the pattern, for we see only in part the great Design. It is to our eyes as a painting done in pointillism. When viewed up close, all one sees is a mass of colorful dots and strokes that have no form or reason to the mind. Yet, as one steps back, into focus comes a vision of shape and form that amazes the eye. Before us stands a meaningful portrait or a beautiful landscape. Our minds could not make reason out of the chaos until we moved away from the canvas and took in the entire picture. So it is with life.

> *And these are but the outer fringe of his works; how faint the whisper we hear of him! Who then can understand the thunder of his power?*
>
> *– Job 26:14*

His councils are not fully spoken, but a gentle whisper within our ear, a transient sound fluttering near then quickly passing away. Compared to the full disclosure of His thundering voice, how could we understand what He speaks if His softly spoken words overwhelm us with His greatness and glory? We as humans are not equipped to apprehend God's words laid bare before us, fully unveiled. Yet, the revealed will of God "teaches and encourages sinners to fear the Lord, and to depart from evil in the exercise of repentance and faith, without desiring to solve all difficulties about the events of this life."[7]

"We see only the outlines, the surface of his mighty doings," a framework of the Great Design of the Master of all things.[8] Yet, we want to understand all these difficulties. Knowledge of the destination encourages us to follow the twists and turns upon the road. Not knowing the result, the reason behind events is difficult for us. We question whether it is worth the struggle. However, who can understand the mystery of God?

> *God understands its way,*
> *And He knows its place.*
> *For He looks to the ends*
> *of the earth,*
> *And sees under the whole*
> *heavens.*
> *~ Job 28:23-24*

Jesus knew His time was coming, so He began to show His disciples that He must go to Jerusalem. "There," spoke Jesus, "I must go and suffer many things from the elders and chief priests and scribes. There I will be killed. Yet there also I will be raised the third day."

Peter's mind reeled with confusion. His heart began to pound, and his breath drew up short. "Killed" he had said. *Not killed. It couldn't be.* Peter took hold of the Master's hand and drew him aside. He began to rebuke Jesus, saying, "Far be it from You, Lord; this shall not happen to You!"

Jesus sighed and His heart sank in disappointment. He turned and looked at Peter, knowing this impetuous disciple did not understand. The pull of His humanity tugged at Jesus, for He knew what was to come, and He feared what He would have to suffer. Suddenly Jesus cried out, "Get behind Me, Satan! You are an offense to Me, for you are not mindful of the things of God, but the things of men."

Shock and dismay caused Peter to step back as he drew in his breath sharply.

Jesus calmed Himself, then turned to His disciples and spoke softly. "If anyone desires to come after Me, let him deny himself, and take up his cross, and follow Me. For whoever desires to save his life will lose it, but whoever loses his life for My sake will find it." Jesus placed a reassuring hand upon Peter's shoulder and smiled at him. "For what profit is it to a man if he gains the whole world, and loses his own soul? Or what will a man give in exchange for his soul?" (Matthew 16:21-26)

Slowly, Christ reveals to His people the plan He has for their lives. Those who follow Christ should not expect good things from the world, for even Christ did not gain the world, but was condemned by it.

We consider Christ stricken by God, smitten and afflicted. When we suffer, we automatically begin to question God, blaming Him. We see pain and sorrow as a punishment. We see Christ as being punished by God. But we are wrong to think so, for it was not for His sin that He suffered, but our sin. May it be that we suffer, not because of some sin we

> Surely, He has borne our griefs
> And carried our sorrows;
> Yet we esteemed Him stricken,
> Smitten by God, and afflicted.
> But He was wounded for our transgressions,
> He was bruised for our iniquities;
> The chastisement for our peace was upon Him,
> And by His stripes we are healed.
> – Isaiah 53: 4-5

have committed, but because of someone else's sin. We want to turn our face away from the suffering Savior, yet the very thing that we abhor to see, is the very greatest of His gifts to us, the most important part of His work. The very thing that brings us such sorrow in this world may be the greatest and most important part of our work here on earth.

Patiently, Jesus endured the sufferings of this world for the greater joy of our salvation. So too, we are called to share in this passion. "The spirit of Christianity always enables a man to bear the ills of life with patience; to receive death with joy; and to expect, by faith, the resurrection of the body, and the life of the world to come."9

Like Job, I have followed the path that God has laid out for me. I have done all that I could to keep His ways. His words, I have treasured more than nourishment for my body. But God is unique and He does not change, for nothing can deter Him from His will. *Whatever His soul desires, that He does.* Who can stand against God? The Lord performs all that He has appointed. He even allows darkness to enter my life; therefore, I fear what He has in store for me, for I am weak and He is mighty. (Job 23:11-17) Yet, He knows the path that is set before my feet. He does not leave me forsaken, but tries me in the fire. I will emerge refined.

When I am teaching my children, they often complain, "Why do we have to do this?" I tell them that they have to trust me, that there is method in my madness, that I know where this is taking them. They must have faith that I know what I am doing. In the same way, we

> *But He knows the way that I take; When He has tested me, I shall come forth as gold.*
> - Job 23:10

must trust God. There is a purpose to what happens in our lives.

We must have faith that God knows what He is doing, that He knows where this will take us.

It is easy to accept the good that God gives us, but can we accept the bad? When we become a Christian, we are to surrender our will to the Will of God. We are to be "living sacrifices." (Romans 12:1) So then, are we willing to allow God to do with us what He will, knowing that this may mean being led down a difficult path? Can we say as Jesus did, "Not My will, but Yours be done." (Luke 22:42) But we do have an assurance that all things will work together for good, we just may not always see that *good* for a time. Ultimately though, to be in God's will is the best place to be. Remember, wherever we go, whatever we do, God is with us.

> For you are the temple of the living God. As God has said: "I will dwell in them And walk among them. I will be their God, And they shall be My people."
> ~ 2 Corinthians 6:16

One of my father's favorite songs was "His Eye Is on the Sparrow." He often sang it in church, filling the sanctuary with his deep bass voice. His voice was so deep that the floorboards rumbled under our feet. When the author of the beautiful words was asked where she received her inspiration, she related this story.

When visiting Mr. and Mrs. Doolittle in Elmira, New York, in the spring of 1905, Civilla Martin and her husband were struck by the Doolittle's *bright hopefulness* despite the physical limitations they had endured. Mrs. Doolittle had been bedridden for the past twenty years. Her husband was confined to a wheelchair. Despite their difficulties, the two lived cheerful Christian lives, often conveying comfort and inspiration to all they knew. Dr. Martin inquired about the secret to the couple's happy disposition. "Mrs.

Doolittle's reply was simple: 'His eye is on the sparrow, and I know He watches me.' The beauty of this simple expression of boundless faith gripped the hearts and fired the imagination of Dr. Martin and me." Out of this experience sprung the beautiful hymn, "His Eye Is on the Sparrow."[10]

When we sink in the mire of life, when we cannot struggle any longer, that is when we fall before the throne and give it all to God. The way is narrow and often a foot slips off the path and into the slough on the side of the road. Even so, "Why should I be discouraged... Though by the path He leadeth, but one step I may see; His eye is on the sparrow, and I know He watches me."[11] With that assurance I walk, though the way may be difficult and I see no way out, though the light is hidden, I take the next step in faith.

Life is for the living, so we move on. For joy comes in the morning. When the night of sorrow ends, we find joy. It is okay to have joy again. That does not mean the grief is gone. A part of me will always be back there grieving. A part of me died that day. But healing does take place. Years have passed, and though I look with hope to the future, I occasionally lapse back into the pit of despair. Then I seek my Savior. He is always there waiting to pull me out again. He is my Tower of Strength.

## Episode 12

# FOR SUCH A TIME

*Rejoicing in hope, patient in tribulation, continuing*
*steadfastly in prayer.*

*~ Romans 12:12*

I can feel it, creeping up on me, as a cloud gathering in the north moving upon a cold breeze. The grief bears heavy upon me still as my momentum fails and I slip down the spiral. Ever is it hovering, waiting to devour, reaching with gloomy fingers to entangle. It's not an easy thing. When the initial shock of September 11 began to fade, and the feelings broke through the numbness, I felt overcome. The weight was so heavy that I would cry out to God, "Don't ask this of me. I cannot do it. It's too big. I cannot carry it." And I wondered, "How did it come to this?"

The soul grows so heavy it is as though tears drop from it like rain upon a rooftop. Steady, slowly, the silent droplets fall. Tolkien wrote, "The sound of mourning was woven into the themes

> *My soul is weary with sorrow; strengthen me according to Your word.*
> *~ Psalm 119:28*

of the world."[1] It is, according to Tolkien, the sorrow of the "long defeat," which is interwoven into the tapestry of all life. This defeat is the defeat of evil, but it is seen as long and painful, and all carry it with them as they journey into the quest for spiritual truth, the quest that brings them home, and to a better understanding of who they really are. Suffering is an Evil beyond the power of man. Yet, God is able to bring Good out of the works of Evil, and while suffering is difficult to bear, if embraced in its full understanding and accepted, can bring the bearer "pity and endurance in hope." Through suffering, strength is brought to the spirit and sorrow is turned to wisdom.[2]

"Now as Jesus passed by, He saw a man who was blind from birth. And His disciples asked Him, saying, "Rabbi, who sinned, this man or his parents, that he was born blind?

> *He does great things*
> *past finding out,*
> *Yes, wonders*
> *without number.*
> *- Job 9:10*

"Jesus answered, 'Neither this man nor his parents sinned, but that the works of God should be revealed in him.'" (John 9:1-3)

So for what cause do men suffer in this world? The blind man had done nothing to inherit his blindness, yet here he was, blind. Our human nature insists there must be a cause and that someone is at fault. Yet, here Jesus says that no one was the cause, but that the works of God may be revealed in him; that the glory of God's Son may shine through this man's healing.

I love the story of Esther. Here is a beautiful tale of bravery and sacrifice. Esther, a young Jewish girl, was taken into the harem of the king of Persia to be his wife. Through betrayals and intrigue, Haman, the king's second in command, plotted against the Jewish people living in Persia, tricking the king into signing a decree to have all the people of Jewish descent killed on a certain day. Now the king, being unaware that indeed Esther was a Jew, sealed the decree into law. It then fell upon Esther to save her people, but in order to do this, she must appear unsummoned before the king, a crime punishable by death. To make matters worse, her relationship with the king had deteriorated. She no longer had the assurance that the king was pleased with her. How could she muster the courage when death was almost certain?

Mordecai, Esther's cousin, an official in the king's court sent a message to Esther who he had raised as his own child. "Do not think in your heart that you will escape in the king's palace any more than all the other Jews. For if you remain completely silent at this time, relief and deliverance will arise for the Jews from another place, but you and your father's house will perish. Yet, who knows whether you have come to the kingdom for such a time as this?" (Esther 4: 12-14)

*For such a time as this.* The words run through my mind repeatedly, ebbing and flowing as a wave upon the shore. How profound. Everything that has happened in our lives could be preparing us *for such a time as this*, the good, the bad, all of it. Esther was taken from her home by force, made the queen to a tyrannical king, then burdened with the survival of her very race at the price of her own life. All these events were terrible, yet here we see God's Providence working in her life, laying out each step in order to provide salvation for her people. Yet, as Mordecai reveals, Esther still had free will to choose to do nothing. God will save His people with or without her, for if she chooses not to lay down her life, another will rise up to do the work of God.

God has a plan for our lives, a path He foresees as the best way to fulfill His plan of salvation for His people. Yet we have a choice whether we take the path or go down another road. Either way, God's plan will be accomplished. The question is whether we will be a part of it.

Mordecai tells Esther that if she does not do this, if she does not help her people, but tries to preserve her own life, she will lose it anyway, for she cannot escape what lay ahead. Neither can we escape what lays ahead for humanity on that Great Day. Would it not be better to suffer for a time in this world so that we can gain the next?

So what did Esther choose? With love and bravery, she stood tall, saying, "I will go to the king, which is against the law; and if I perish, I perish!" (Esther 4:16) And as the story unfolds, we see that the king's heart softened toward Esther, and he granted her petition. Through the course of events, Esther's faithfulness brought salvation to her people and ultimately salvation for all people.

> See, from His head,
> His hands, His feet,
> Sorrow and love flow
> mingled down;
> Did e'er such love and
> sorrow meet,
> Or thorns compose so
> rich a crown?
> ~ Isaac Watts[3]

Often we find ourselves in situations that seem all wrong. Everything seems so big and we are so small. How can I do anything that can influence the world? I am only one person of no consequence, with no voice. Who am I that anyone even takes notice? Yet, here I find myself in a situation that is so much bigger than I am. God often raises up the most unlikely people in the most unimaginably bleak environments to play strategic roles in the unfolding drama of salvation history. After all, who really were the heroes of the past, except common men and women who were caught in events that propelled them into greatness? Most of the time, these people did not choose to be in the situations in which they found themselves, yet they took on the challenge for the good that needed to be accomplished.

It's all wrong. By rights we shouldn't even be here.

But we are. It's like in the great stories… the ones that really mattered. Full of darkness and danger they were. 'Cause sometimes you didn't want to know the end because how could the end be happy? How can the world go back to the way it was when so much bad had happened? But in the end it's only a passing thing. A shadow even darkness must pass. A new day will come and when the sun shines it will shine out the clearer. Those were the stories that stayed with you, that meant something, even if you were too small to understand why. But… I do understand. I know now. Folks in those stories had lots of chances in turning back, only they didn't. They kept going because they were holding on to something… That there's some good left in this world… and it's worth fighting for.

*~ The Two Towers*[4]

When we meet our Lord Jesus will He not say, "See here My hands, My feet, My side. I have been wounded for you. Now show me your wounds."

Will we say, "Lord, see here, I have none to show You."

Then He will say, "My child, was there nothing worth fighting for?"[5]

As we traveled by car to Virginia that night of September 11, 2001, the skies were silent, empty, and dark. The amazing thing about the night sky without airplanes, the stars are more notable. As I look back now, I can see it was as though the magnificence of God's majesty shined the brighter for the lack of man's influence upon the heavens. Beyond this world, there lies goodness that

115

cannot be touched by evil.

Do we do nothing? Do we let Evil win? Or do we fight? It seems at times that it is of no use. That there is nothing left to fight for. But there is good and beauty out there that no evil can touch, and it is worth fighting for.

One evening I was visiting with a patient of mine who was dying of cancer. She was a beautiful Christian woman. I was having difficulty accepting that God was not healing her. She

> Far above the Ephel-Duath in the West the night-sky was still dim and pale. There, peeping among the cloud-wrack above a dark tor high up in the mountains, Sam saw a white star twinkle for a while. The beauty of it smote his heart, as he looked up out of the forsaken land, and hope returned to him. For like a shaft, clear and cold, the thought pierced him that in the end the Shadow was only a small and passing thing: there was light and high beauty forever beyond its reach.
>
> ~ J. R. R. Tolkien[6]

asked if I would read to her from the Bible. I agreed and asked her what she would like to hear. She did not care; she just wanted to hear the Word of God. I randomly opened the Bible, and it fell open at Isaiah 57. I began to read:

> *The righteous perishes,*
> *And no man takes it to heart;*
> *Merciful men are taken away,*
> *While no one considers*
> *That the righteous is taken away from evil.*
> *He shall enter into peace;*
> *They shall rest in their beds,*
> *Each one walking in his uprightness.*
> ~ Isaiah 57:1-2

Was it by chance that the scriptures opened to that chapter of Isaiah? Or was God teaching me? My patient died on Mother's Day that year. Gently, she slipped into the next life. Watching her those few months as she journeyed the path of death, I saw that death is not always a negative. She was ready to be with the Lord. Life had grown weary and

> Among the tales of sorrow and of ruin... there are yet some in which amid weeping there is joy and under the shadow of death light that endures.
> ~ J. R. R. Tolkien[7]

painful. And she really wasn't dead after all, her spirit lives on in the presence of her Blessed Savior.

The main theme that runs through the works of Tolkien is death. Mortality is "a mystery of God which no more is known than that 'what God has proposed for Men is hidden,' a grief and an envy to the immortal."[8] Death is their fate, the gift to Men from God, yet the Evil one has "cast a shadow upon it, and confounded it with darkness, and brought forth evil out of good, and fear out of hope."[9] Evil divides us, causing us to fear death, troubling us with the thought of our mortality. Man's mortality is seen by Tolkien as "freedom from the circles of the world."[10] Retaining men to the confines of the world would be withholding from them the Gift given by God, the gift of rest from the struggles of this present world. "Therefore [He] willed that the hearts of Men should seek beyond the world and should find no rest therein; but they should have a virtue to shape their life, amid the powers and chances of the world,... which is as fate to all things else..."[11]

We rest not while we are in this world. Our souls long for the world beyond. God has placed something in us that seeks after a Creator. There is a void in our Being when we do not know God. Yet, we still love this life, and hold onto it, all the while we hope for the world to come. So then, God has granted Men freedom to choose his own fate. Each choice presents a result, which must be lived with, a result that affects not only the one choosing, but often others as well.

Threads of salvation message are in the writings of Tolkien. "For there is one loyalty from which no man can be absolved in heart for any cause... But it is for mercy upon Men and their deliverance from... the Deceiver that I would plead, since some at least have remained faithful. And as for the Ban, I will suffer in myself the penalty, lest all my people should become guilty."[12]

Christ has taken the penalty for men so that the curse of the broken blood oath be not placed upon them. So in the suffering of the Savior, Men have been given the Hope that comes out of Death. And "in the deep places [He] gives thought to music great and terrible; and the echo of that music runs through all the veins of the world in sorrow

> For us is required a blind trust, and a hope without assurance, knowing not what lies before us in a little while... But this we hold to be true, that [our] home is not here,... nor anywhere within the Circles of this World. And the Doom of Men, that they should depart, was at first a gift... It became a grief to them only because coming under the shadow of [Evil] it seemed to them that they were surrounded by a great darkness, of which they were afraid; and some grew willful and proud and would not yield, until life was reft from them.
> ~ J. R. R. Tolkien[14]

and in joy; for if joyful is the fountain that rises in the sun, its springs are in the wells of sorrow unfathomed at the foundations of the Earth."[13] Our joy, our hope is founded in the suffering of Christ who was marked by God for this purpose before the making of the world. (1 Peter 1:20)

While we may not know fully what awaits us, we do have an assurance that what is waiting for us on the other side is beyond anything we could comprehend. Its magnificence and beauty are beyond our desire. The promise holds that our "Doom" is a glorious reward where death and evil cannot touch us. Why then do we grieve for those who go on before us? We grieve for our want of them. The loss of their life has left us with a void. It pushes into our face the thought of our own mortality, and the fear of what lays ahead troubles us. So we grieve. We cling to the memory of their loss and the thought of that grief, grieves us more. At times, the grief becomes the only thread that holds them to this earth. By clutching onto our grief, we grasp the last thread of their existence on earth. If we let go, they are gone. So we carry the shadow of pain in our hearts. I wonder, do people see that shadow in my eyes?

> For that woe is past... and I would take what joy is here left, untroubled by memory. And maybe there is woe enough yet to come, though still hope may seem bright.
>
> ~ J. R. R. Tolkien[15]

Tolkien knew that when you grieve, you have to let the person go in order to heal. He also knew that was easier said than done. In the film version of *The Return of the King*, director Peter Jackson added to Tolkien's sentiment. As King Théoden lay dying from his wounds, Éowyn knelt beside him saying that she was going to save him. The king looked gently upon Éowyn as he said, "My body is broken... you have to let me go."

How do you find it in yourself to let go? I don't know how to do this. How do I let my father go when all I have of him is my grief?

119

# Episode 13

# RESOLUTION

*He uncovers deep things out of darkness,*
*And brings the shadow of death to light.*

*~Job 12:22*

When I was in high school, my sister and my father were in a car accident. Thankfully, the two of them only suffered minor injuries, but the car was totaled. Going back to the scene, we could see how God had protected them from harm. Miraculously, my father had been able to steer the car to the side of the road, maneuvering between two signposts so their car was only side swiped instead of being hit head-on. What made it miraculous was the space between the two signs was only large enough for the car to slide in sideways, in a way that was impossible for a car. How then did the car manage to slip in between the signs without even knocking into the poles? We were all awed by God's great protection.

Yet the accident traumatized my sister, and she was fearful to get behind the wheel of a car. My father told her, "I'll give you three days to recover, then you have to get behind the wheel again. You cannot let anything or anyone have dominion over you, but God." Somewhere, I planted that advice in my mind. After September 11, those words kept coming to me. I had to live up to them. This will not have dominion over me. God will.

Suffering is a universal condition. It falls on the good, the bad, and the innocent, for we are a fallen race and it is the condition we now hold. God does not distinguish between the good and the bad; He sends sun and rain upon both their heads. (Matthew 5:45) If God had not loved us while we were enemies, how would we have been saved? If good happens to the bad, does it not follow that bad also happens to those who are good?

> *With Him are strength and prudence. The deceived and the deceiver are His.*
> ~ Job 12:16

Tragedy shook this nation. The events of September 11, the loss of so many innocent lives cries out for retribution. But justice does not always come in this world. My father often replied to our cries that *it* wasn't fair with, "Whoever said life would be fair?" Life is not fair. So again, I quote Tolkien:

> Many that live deserve death. And some that die deserve life. Can you give it to them? Then do not be too eager to deal out death in judgement. For even the very wise cannot see all ends.
> ~ J. R. R. Tolkien[1]

Justice is the Providence of God. At times, it seems God smiles upon the wicked, granting them safety and prosperity while the just suffer and die. But the deceivers of this world are God's; therefore, He is aware of what they do, and he knows their ways. He may allow them to abide for a time, yet He will reward them for their enterprises. Their day will come when the vengeance of God will rain down upon them in the proper course of Time. God grants the wicked a space of time in order to provide them opportunity for repentance, for God wishes that none should perish. (2 Peter 3:9) This is hard for us as humans to comprehend, for we want revenge upon those who injure us. But God is Perfect Love. He sees beyond the corruption of sin into the potential faithfulness of the lost. Glad we should be, for if it were not so, where would we be today?

> He gives them security,
> and they rely on it;
> Yet His eyes are on
> their ways.
> They are exalted for a
> little while,
> Then they are gone.
> They are brought low;
> They are taken out of
> the way like all others;
> They dry out like the
> heads of grain.
> - Job 24:23-24

As a nation, we have asked God to leave our schools, then we complain when He is not there. We asked Him to leave our government, and complain when He is not present. Then when disaster strikes, we censure God, because He did not prevent it. God is not going to force His will upon us, for this would be overriding our free will. He will not dwell where He is not wanted. We can't have it both ways.

Throughout the turbulent history of the Israelites, God's Presence rested upon the Mercy Seat of the Ark of the Covenant, within the Holy of Holies of the Temple. So magnificent was the radiance of His Glory that to be in its presence unsummoned was certain death to the beholder. The departure of the Shekinah, which happened several times in the Old Testament, marked God's displeasure with His people. When the Israelites turned away from God, when they broke their blood oath and worshiped other gods instead, God removed His Presence from among them as He deemed He was no longer wanted. When a people no longer desire the Lord's presence, He leaves. (Deuteronomy 31:17-18)

The loss of God's Shekinah, though, denotes the grave consequences of the removal of His blessing and protection. Unfortunately, the just often are swept away by the downfall of a nation as Daniel did when the Babylonian Empire captured the Israelites.

> God who gave us life gave us liberty. And can the liberties of a nation be thought secure when we have removed their only firm basis, a conviction in the minds of the people that these liberties are of the Gift of God?
> – Thomas Jefferson[2]

I have a fear that God will give our nation what it asks, and His presence, His Shekinah will depart. Surely, it is just a few who desire our nation to remove our motto *In God We Trust*, yet if we sit and do nothing, will their will win out? I do not know if the condition we find our country in has anything to do with the events of September 11. I do not pretend to apprehend all the mysteries of God and the unfolding of world events. However, we have enjoyed the protection of Providence throughout the founding of this nation. Any student of history can tell you how, at just the right time, the forces of nature often intervened during battle on behalf of our country resulting in victory.

> Do not fear those who kill the body but cannot kill the soul. But rather fear Him who is able to destroy both soul and body in hell.
> Are not two sparrows sold for a copper coin?
> And not one of them falls to the ground apart from your Father's will.
> But the very hairs of your head are all numbered.
> Do not fear therefore; you are of more value than many sparrows...
> – Matthew 10: 28-31

We read often in scripture that Jesus looked upon the multitude and was moved with compassion for the people, for they were weary and scattered like sheep without a

123

shepherd. So Jesus sent his disciples to tend to the people; He sent them out as sheep among wolves. As the twelve turned to go, Jesus gave them a warning. He warned them that trouble was coming. That brother would rise up against brother; parents would turn on their children. Beatings and scourging would arise from the people within the church. Many would despise them for His name's sake. They were not to fear, for Christ would not abandon them. But he who endured to the end would be saved. (Matthew 10:16-22)

> Do not think that I came to bring peace on earth.
> I did not come to bring peace but a sword... He who does not take his cross and follow after Me is not worthy of Me.
> He who finds his life will lose it,
> and he who loses his life for My sake will find it.
> -Matthew 10: 34, 38-39

Do not be deceived, earth is a spiritual battleground. The battle is here and now. Unfortunately, the innocent and the righteous are often caught in the crossfire. We alone are not enough to defeat the Enemy, but we have the Sword of the Spirit within our grasp. We are promised that as we, God's church, fight, "the gates of Hell shall not prevail against it." (Matthew 16:18). This is a call to arms. This verse does not imply that evil is besieging the tabernacle of God. It says that the *gates of Hell shall not prevail.* In other words, the gates of this world will not stand against us, God's people. It is a picture of forces storming a fortress, battering down the castle gate. We are not to stand and defend ourselves as we stay behind our walls, cowering as we wait to be attacked. We are to storm the fortress of darkness; to go out and fight for what is right.

The battle is not a fight against men. We are battling against "principalities, against powers, against the rulers of the darkness of this age, against spiritual hosts of wickedness in the heavenly places." (Ephesians 6:12) It is a battle against evil, darkness, and hatred, against the enemy of men's souls. The terrorists are simply a symptom of this evil. We are walking behind enemy lines, for the world is the domain of the Enemy. Yet, we cannot fight hate with hate. (Matthew 5:43-48) If we hate then we have let the enemy into our ranks.

> Other evils there are that may come; for [he] is himself but a servant or emissary. Yet it is not our part to master all the tides of this world, but to do what is in us for the succor of those years wherein we are set, uprooting the evil in the fields that we know, so that those who live after may have clean earth to till. What weather they shall have is not ours to rule.
>
> ~ J. R. R. Tolkien[3]

We often hear that the victory is won. And yes, it has been. Christ won when he conquered sin and death. (Colossians 2:13-15) However, if we think the battle is over, we are dead wrong. If the battle were over, Christ would have returned to take us home, and the world would cease. But it hasn't and the Lord still tarries.

Who then will fight the battle?

We fight the battle in our own hearts and minds, in the hearts and minds of our children. We cannot allow the stress of our busy lives to distract us from the fight. Do not put down your arms or the enemy will sneak in and destroy you. A good soldier must array himself with his full armor and don his weapon daily or be vulnerable to attack. We cannot afford to be slack in this, even in the small stuff. Keep watch lest you fall into the hands of the adversary. (Deuteronomy 4:9)

You may say, "But I have no time. I have so much to do."

The enemy will have no pity on you. He will use everything to his advantage. Make the time. The enemy comes as a thief, to steal, to kill and destroy. (John 10:10) He is an accuser that stands before the Judge condemning. Of course, the way is going to be difficult and there will be casualties. The enemy of our souls comes to steal our spirit. If he cannot have our souls, he

> Be sober, be vigilant; because your adversary the devil walks about like a roaring lion, seeking whom he may devour.
>
> ~ 1 Peter 5:8

wishes to silence our voice, for as we live, we bring others to the Lord by our example. Many saints of God have died for this cause, unfairly losing their lives for their faith. The victims of September 11 are such martyrs, as they died for the Christian views of their nation. My own father is now numbered with the martyrs of Christ.

Why has God allowed the martyrs all through time to suffer and die for His cause? Did the Enemy silence their voices even as he killed them? Amazing as it may seem, the more the church is persecuted, the greater the voice of the slain ring out. Hatred cannot stamp it out. Oppression cannot silence it. Persecution turns more to Christ than the quiet worship of believers. We do not know what affect our lives will have on those around us or on those who follow after us. Was it not Saul who held the cloaks of the very men who stoned Stephen, not only witnessing the brutal attack upon this beloved saint but also condoning their actions with pious pleasure? As Saul looked on, he saw Stephen's "face as the face of an angel." (Acts 6:15) After committing himself to God, Stephen fell asleep and died as the first Christian martyr recorded in history. (Acts 6:8-8:1) This very man Saul, who later was called Paul, after meeting our Lord Jesus Christ upon the road to Damascus, (Acts 9:1-19) his heart being ripened by the example of Stephen, became the most influential of all the apostles for the cause of Christ. What if the martyrs had given up? What if we fail the test? What if I fail the test? By being faithful to the end, we prepare the soil for those who will follow.

Over time, a rock in a river is worn down into a beautiful, perfect smooth stone. All the rough edges are worn away. But this cannot be accomplished without first being tried in the turbulent waters. Time and trouble wash over us to wear away our rude, unfinished surfaces. The process is uncomfortable, like sandpaper across skin. We mustn't let the billows of life overtake us, but overcome them, for we

> *Who shall separate us from the love of Christ? Shall tribulation, or distress, or persecution, or famine, or nakedness, or peril, or sword?*
> – Romans 8:35

are more than conquerors. Stand fast in your faith, for nothing can keep you from loving Him who first loved you. (1 John 4:19) If we stand firm in our resolve, nothing anyone can do will annul the payment that was made for us through Christ Jesus.

It is written that for the sake of Christ "we are accounted as sheep for the slaughter." (Romans 8:36) Yet, there is nothing, "neither death nor life nor angels nor principalities nor powers, nor things present nor things to come, nor height nor depth, nor any other created thing, shall be able to separate us from the love of God." (Romans 8:38-39)

> *What then shall we say to these things? If God is for us, who can be against us? He who did not spare His own Son, but delivered Him up for us all, how shall He not with Him also freely give us all things?*
> – Romans 8:31-32

Who then shall we fear? For greater is He who is in us than he who is in the world. (1 John 4:4) So we are more than conquerors, more than victors. We are not only overcoming the enemy in battle, but we are being strengthened in our faith. We have gained endurance in the race toward the goal. It is not by our own strength, but by Him who is in us (Galatians 2:20), that we gain the victory completely and steadfastly. For He, who reached down to the very place of our destruction, has not withheld His mercy, but grasped us and lifted us out.

For this very purpose, Christ came. The Redeemer has come with the balm of anointing, to bind up the broken and heal the wounded, to claim those who were lost, freeing them from the captivity of sin and death. He has come to heal my broken heart, to release me from the bonds of sorrow, to comfort me as I mourn, and to provide for me as I grieve. Christ has for me "a crown of beauty instead of ashes, the oil of gladness instead of mourning, and a garment of praise instead of a spirit of despair." (Isaiah 61: 1-3)

So if we suffer for a time in this world, we cannot compare it with the glory that is to follow. We know that all creation "groans and labors with birth pangs" even until now. Yet, we eagerly await the redemption proffered to us, being "saved in hope, but hope that is seen is not hope; for why does one still hope for what he sees?" Our Hope is for what we do not see; but for the expectation of future glory, we eagerly

> End? Our journey doesn't end here. Death is just another path… One that we all must take. The grey rain curtain of this world rolls back… and all turns to silver glass. And then you see it… White shores… and beyond. The far green country under a swift sunrise.
>
> - *Return of the King*[4]

await with endurance. (Romans 8:18-25) Do not continue grieving over much for those who have fallen asleep, that is those who are dead, as others do who have no hope. They are not utterly lost, for if one believes on the name of Jesus, that He died and rose again, they have the blessed assurance of the resurrection to eternal life. When the clouds are rolled back, we will meet them in the sky, "and thus we shall always be with the Lord. Therefore comfort one another with these words." (1 Thessalonians 4: 13-18)

Let us learn something from our sorrow so that those lost will not have died in vain. As we gaze upon the passage of years, the hourglass turns scattering its sand upon the deeps of time, marking its swift cadence, revealing what has passed and declaring what will come. While life leads us down the path that cannot be traversed again, we tread along

> And let us not grow weary while doing good, for in due season we shall reap if we do not lose heart.
> – Galatians 6:9

laying down the way for those who follow, the field thus sown for the harvest of the young. And though life tries us, His blessings do abound. Through all, yet still we stand, our lives within the Master's hands. There is no going back but forward we climb to new heights, the metrical duration of a single note amidst the orchestration of eternity.

Episode 14

# EVEN SO

*Alas! There are some wounds*
*that cannot be wholly cured.*

*~ J. R. R. Tolkien[1]*

Echoing whispers of the past press forward as the brush of soft shadows of what used to be touch our mind. Life trudges on its path through memories in the making, lingering for a moment, then continuing in its trek. There is no going back. "The wound aches, and the memory of darkness is heavy on me... it will not seem the same; for I shall not be the same. I am wounded with... a long burden. Where shall I find rest?" (Tolkien)[2] It is what it is. No amount of struggle can change anything that has happened. So then, what are we to do, for the wounds cannot be mended and the path cannot be trod anew?

We are to go on. Though darkness lies behind, we turn our backs to it, never to wrestle with it again. Yet, when our thoughts return for a moment to the remembrance of those lost, we linger for a time, relishing the lives that have touched ours. Then we turn back to the westward call of our hearts, for we believe that there we shall find Light. We do not wholly lay aside the memory of those who sleep, but we can emulate the lives of those lost. We can be a testimony to their memory. We can live our lives so as to cry out that our loved ones did not live and die in vain, that their lives mattered and the world is a better place for them having been in it.

Like sheep, Christians obey Christ, their Shepherd. Not only this, but they hear His voice. Knowing Him, they imitate Him and follow Him, wherever He may lead them, yielding to His guidance, trusting in His Providence. To them that follow, He gives eternal life. They shall never perish, but be with Him, safe, for no one can snatch them out of His hand. (John 10: 27-28)

What testimony is there if we serve God when everything is going our way? Will we stand against the billows of Darkness when it comes, or shall we fall into Shadow? When the slings and arrows of this world rise up against us, will we stand firm? Do we let the Deceiver twist the words of God so that he can use them against us as he stands beside us to accuse us before God? Can we say as the songwriter says, that "Whatever my lot, Thou hast taught me to say, Even so, it is well with my soul?"[3]

Horatio Spafford penned those words after suffering a great loss. His law business failed following the Great Chicago fire. Shortly after, his young son died at the age

> Though the fig tree may not blossom,
> Nor fruit be on the vines;
> Though the labor of the olive may fail,
> And the fields yield no food;
> Though the flock may be cut off from the fold,
> And there be no herd in the stalls—
> Yet I will rejoice in the LORD,
> I will joy in the God of my salvation.
> The LORD God is my strength;
> He will make my feet like deer's feet,
> And He will make me walk on my high hills.
> ~ Habakkuk 3:17-19

of four. Planning to spend some time in Europe, Horatio put his entire family on a ship bound for England. He remained behind to finish some business concerns. News reached him that the ship had collided with another and sunk. His wife sent a message, "Survived alone." All of his children were dead. As he traveled by ship to meet his grieving wife, the ship passed the place where his daughters had perished. He was moved to write the words to this inspired hymn, "It Is Well With My Soul."[4]

Though we suffer, if we believe we do so for the cause of Christ, we have no need to worry, for Christ is able to keep us unto the very end. There is no other that we can have so much confidence in to deliver us out of our sorrow. (2 Timothy 1:12)

> *Though He slay me,*
> *yet will I trust Him.*
> *~ Job 13:15*

I was sitting in church one day listening to a sermon. I do not remember what the pastor was preaching, but I remember sitting there and being overwhelmed with a sense of God's love for me. The thought came to me with a strong determination that no matter what had happened, as my sorrow and pain were multiplied, even so, I would serve the Lord. I would meet those issues head-on, and though I suffered, I would stand firm in my resolve, fixed on my intent to place my trust in God. (Job 13:15) For I know that my Redeemer lives and He has purchased me. And when my flesh has failed, I too will be transformed, and I will see Him face to face. (Job 19:25-27) How this fills the heart with joy even in the throes of suffering, for that Hope yearns within my soul, and I can rejoice even in sorrow.

I do not understand why events unfolded as they did. I do not know why I have been chosen to walk this path. I hurt and relief comes slowly. Yet, still I stand. Even so, I will serve the Lord in faith and in truth, trusting in His divine judgment. As David did, so too will I. I will let the Lord work out the details in His time. I will simply walk the path in the light that has been given me.

Are we ready to meet the trials of life head-on? Our love for God should not be conditional. Though at times I do not understand what God is doing, even though I feel let down, and disappointed, I have a hope and a trust that the Lord knows the outcome. I have

> *I will stand my watch*
> *And set myself on the rampart,*
> *And watch to see what He*
> *will say to me,*
> *And what I will answer when*
> *I am corrected.*
> *- Habakkuk 2:1*

a determination to see this life through for I have an investment in heaven.

In the integrity of my father before me, I stand firm in my resolve to let no one or anything have dominion over me but God. So I wait on the Lord.

As I stand on the brink of a new day, looking to the east as the golden orb opens her eye above the horizon; I feel her warmth upon my face. Her radiant beams reach out across the skies and chase the dark of night away. So too I stand and wait upon God's Son as He illuminates my new day with His warmth and love. And so I place my trust in Him, the Keeper of life, the Strength of my soul.

Life continues, the young grow, the seasons pass, yet one is missing. But he waits for me. I will join him in glorious reunion. His life has been a testimony of faith for me to follow. He lived his Silent Resolve. So I face a new day as I "haul up the morning" and though the morning may seem distant, I stand firm knowing that the night must always give way to the dawn.

The books will be balanced—but not in our time, in God's time.

*For the vision is yet for an appointed time;*
*But at the end it will speak, and it will not lie.*
*Though it tarries, wait for it;*
*Because it will surely come,*
*It will not tarry.*

~ Habakkuk 2:3

# Episode 15

# EPILOGUE

*There is a tide in the affairs of men,*
*Which, taken at the flood, leads on to fortune;*
*Omitted, all the voyage of their life*
*Is bound in shallows, and in miseries.*

*~Shakespeare[1]*

Light and shadow dance upon my mind mingling with thoughts of past and future. As the curtain is drawn over the past, we look back through the veil to see what was, to learn and grow from what has been and to prepare for the times to come. Then we turn and face the future looming brightly in the distance like a sunrise cresting in the east glowing red over the horizon, promising a clear day and a bright sun that bears its heat upon our face, warming us, and chasing night away.

As the morning breath exhales upon this new day, reflections of the past linger within the mind, enabling one to pause briefly and look into the past and measure the events, hoping to find a pleasing history. It is our history that is examined, the joys and sorrows, always striving to enlighten and look beyond what seems difficult. Time passes without a rearward glance, without a care as to what is being left behind. So we remember, a record, so that none will forget what was accomplished and what was experienced. But always together, with those who love us, we strive in the world, and that alone can make it a better place.

Recently, I heard a pastor say, "Why do we struggle? The struggle really isn't ours. It is the Lord's battle, so why are we trying to fight it?" The Lord cannot fully take the conflict on until we let go of the turmoil within us. We are simply to be still and know that He is God. (Psalm 46:10) All things will be accomplished in His time. We must release the hold that grasps the last threads of struggle and cling to the promises of the Lord, for the Dawn is approaching.

Sitting here, I write the final words of this book, yet it is not the end of the story. My mother has moved on from her grief, beginning a life with her new husband. My children are growing and preparing for their futures. As I travel with our music ministry, the Van Martins, I am often called upon to give my testimony. Standing before the congregation, my heart warms as I imagine my father looking down from above, watching me. Rising up on his toes, then settling back on his heels as he lands with several bounces, grinning with his arms folded across his chest, he is saying, "How about that." And I know he is pleased.

The dogwood tree that spread its limbs over my father's grave is gone; the hill stands barren, as though my father's spirit is no longer bound to the earth. With the last few strokes of the keyboard, a wave of emotion rolls over me. The tears come. It is as though I am saying my final farewell, cutting the last strings that bind me to my father in this world. Relief and sadness wash over me as I empty myself. Though I will always carry it with me, I am placing a ribbon around my grief, lifting my eyes to the rising Son.

As the dawn approaches, the past is left behind and I turn my face to a new day, looking longingly toward what lies ahead, hoping for the joy and blessings that may rest just beyond the horizon. It is these blessings that I pray will lie in wait for each of you as you journey through life toward the goal. As you travel on, remember that Love came down and claimed us for His own.

What though the radiance which was once so bright
Be now for ever taken from my sight,
Though nothing can bring back the hour
Of Splendor in the grass, of glory in the flower;
We will grieve not, rather find
Strength in what remains behind;
In the primal sympathy
Which having been must ever be;
In the soothing thoughts that spring
Out of human suffering;
In the faith that looks through death,
In years that bring the philosophic mind.

~ William Wordsworth[2]

In loving memory of
Stanley Rylon Hall
April 14, 1933—September 11, 2001

# NOTES

## Dedication

1. Tolkien, J. R. R., *The Two Towers*. (New York: Random House Publishing Group. 1994), 92.

## Preface

1. Shakespeare, William, "Sonnet XXX," *The Complete Works of William Shakespeare*. (New York. Avenel Books. 1975), 1196

## Episode 1 / Forever Changed

1. Tolkien, J. R. R., *Fellowship of the Ring*. (New York: Random House Publishing Group. 1994), 360.
2. *The Lord of the Rings: The Two Towers*, directed by Peter Jackson (USA: New Line Cinema, 2002), Film.
3. Shakespeare, William, "Romeo and Juliet," *The Complete Works of William Shakespeare*. (New York. Avenel Books. 1975), 1035.
4. *The Lord of the Rings: The Return of the King*, directed by Peter Jackson (USA: New Line Cinema, 2003), Film.

## Episode 2 / Awakened

1. Tolkien, J. R. R., *Fellowship of the Ring*. (New York: Random House Publishing Group. 1994), 403.

2. Dickinson, Emily, "The Bustle in a House (1078)," *American Literature for Christian Schools 2nd ed.* (South Carolina: BJU Press. 2003), 416.

3. Tolkien, J. R. R., *Fellowship of the Ring.* (New York: Random House Publishing Group. 1994), 401.

## Episode 3 / Tears

1. Tolkien, J. R. R., *The Return of the King.* (New York: Random House Publishing Group. 1994), 339.

2. Taken from *Growing Strong in the Seasons of Life.* By Charles R. Swindoll, Copyright © 1983 by Charles R. Swindoll, Inc. Use by permission of Zondervan. www.zondervan.com

3. Schönberg, Claude-Michel, "Empty Chairs at Empty Tables." *Les Miserables.* 1980. Lyrics.

4. Milton, John, *Paradise Lost. A Poem in Twelve Books. 2nd ed.* (London: S. Simmons, 1674), lines 254-255.

5. Lewis, C. S., *A Grief Observed.* (New York: Harper San Francisco. 1996), 9-10.

## Episode 4 / Silence

1. *The Lord of the Rings: The Return of the King*, directed by Peter Jackson (USA: New Line Cinema, 2003), Film.

2. Tolkien, J. R. R., *The Letters of J. R. R. Tolkien,* edited by Humphrey Carpenter. (Boston: Houghton Mifflin Company. 1981), 347.

## Episode 5 / Seeking After His Sheep

1. From "There Is a River," Words & Music by Max & David Sapp © All rights reserved. International copyright secured.

2. *The Lord of the Rings: The Fellowship of the Ring*, directed by Peter Jackson. (USA: New Line Cinema, 2001), Film.

3. Ibid.

## Episode 6 / Through the Veil

1. Tolkien, J. R. R., *Fellowship of the Ring*. (New York: Random House Publishing Group. 1994), 420.

## Episode 7 / Silent Resolve

1. Association of Old Crows (AOC). *Business Development Award*. Copyright © 2010-2011, AOC. All Rights Reserved. Web. 21 Oct. 2011.
2. Ibid.
3. Ibid.
4. Ibid.

## Episode 8 / The Face of Evil

1. Lewis, C. S., *A Grief Observed*. (New York: Harper San Francisco. 1996), 56.
2. Tolkien, J. R. R., *Fellowship of the Ring*. (New York: Random House Publishing Group. 1994), 65.
3. Keats, John. "Sonnet XIV Address to the Same." *The Complete Poems of John Keats*. (New York: Random House, Inc. 1994), 33.
4. Tolkien, J. R. R., *The Return of the King*. (New York: Random House Publishing Group. 1994), 158.
5. Editors Philip Schaff, DD, LLD and Henry Wace, DD, *A Select Library Nicene and Post-Nicene Fathers of the Christian Church Vol. 1* (New York: The Christian Literature Company. 1890), 129.
6. Goldsworthy, Adrian, *How Rome Fell*. (New Haven and London: Yale University Press. 2009), 96.
7. Coolidge, Olivia, *Lives of Famous Romans*. (Boston: Houghton Mifflin Company. 1965), 125.
8. Ibid, 202-208.

9. Bush, President George W. "The World Will Always Remember September 11." (East Room at the White House. December 11, 2001), Speech.

## Episode 9 / Not Alone

1. Barnes, Albert, *Barnes' Notes on the* New *Testament.* (New York: Harper and Brothers. 1849), 199.
2. Henry, Matthew, *Matthew Henry's Concise Commentary on the Whole Bible.* (Tennessee: Thomas Nelson Publishers. 1997), 1236.
3. Hall, Randall, interview with Ben Kieffer. The Exchange. Copyright @ Iowa Public Radio. 9 September 2011. Broadcast.
4. Tolkien, J. R. R., *The Return of the King.* (New York: Random House Publishing Group. 1994), 148.
5. Gilbert, Josiah H., *Dictionary of Burning Words of Brilliant Writers.* (New York: Wilbur B. Ketchum. 1895), 567.
6. From "Through It All," Copyright 2011 Andraè Crouch.
7. Wesley, John, *Explanatory Notes Upon the New Testament. Vol. II.* (London: Thomas Cordeux. 1819), 311.
8. Heavenly Midis Songbook, *Do You Know My Jesus?* (Words and Music by W. F. Lakey and V. B. Ellis Copyright 1957, V. B. Ellis. 29 March 2009), Web. 7 November 2011.

## Episode 10 / God's Sovereignty

1. Henry, Matthew, *Matthew Henry's Concise Commentary on the Whole Bible.* (Tennessee: Thomas Nelson Publishers. 1997), 450.
2. Excerpts from THE SILMARILLION, Second Edition by J. R. R. Tolkien, edited by Christopher Tolkien. Copyright © 1977 by J.R.R. Tolkien Copyright Trust and Christopher Reuel Tolkien. Copyright © 1981 by J. R. R. Tolkien Trust. Copyright © 1999 by Christopher Reuel Tolkien. Used by permission of Houghton Mifflin Harcourt Publishing Company. All rights reserved. 36.

## Episode 11 / All in His Hands

1. ChurchLead, *He Maketh No Mistake*. (A. M. Overton Copyright 1932. 27 January 2011), Web. 7 November 2011.
2. Excerpts from THE SILMARILLION, Second Edition by J. R. R. Tolkien, edited by Christopher Tolkien. Copyright © 1977 by J.R.R. Tolkien Copyright Trust and Christopher Reuel Tolkien. Copyright © 1981 by J. R. R. Tolkien Trust. Copyright © 1999 by Christopher Reuel Tolkien. Used by permission of Houghton Mifflin Harcourt Publishing Company. All rights reserved. 83.
3. From "Is Not this the Land of Beulah." William Hunter. 1884. Copyright: Public Domain
4. Tolkien, J. R. R., *Fellowship of the Ring*. (New York: Random House Publishing Group. 1994), 61.
5. Henry, Matthew, *Matthew Henry's Concise Commentary on the Whole Bible*. (Tennessee: Thomas Nelson Publishers. 1997), 440.
6. Ibid.
7. Ibid, 441.
8. Barnes, Albert, *Notes, Critical, Illustrative, and Practical, On the Book of Job. Vol. 2*. (New York: Leavitt & Company. 1849), 53.
9. Clarke, Adam, *The New Testament: Commentary and Critical Notes, Vol. 1*. (New York: N. Bangs and J. Emory. 1825), 155.
10. Net Hymnal, *His Eye is on the Sparrow*. (Copyright NetHymnal 2000-2011. 7 August 2007), Web. 2 November 2011. http://nethymnal.org/htm/h/i/hiseyeis.htm
11. Ibid.

## Episode 12 / For Such a Time

1. Excerpts from THE SILMARILLION, Second Edition by J. R. R. Tolkien, edited by Christopher Tolkien. Copyright © 1977 by J.R.R. Tolkien Copyright Trust and Christopher Reuel Tolkien. Copyright © 1981 by J. R. R. Tolkien Trust. Copyright © 1999

by Christopher Reuel Tolkien. Used by permission of Houghton Mifflin Harcourt Publishing Company. All rights reserved. 28.

2. Ibid.
3. From "When I Survey the Wondrous Cross," Isaac Watts [1674-1748]. Copyright: Public Domain
4. *The Lord of the Rings: The Two Towers*, directed by Peter Jackson (USA: New Line Cinema, 2002), Film.
5. Oglesby, Enoch H, *Born in the Fire: Case studies in Christian Ethics and Globalization*. (New York: Pilgrim Press. 1990), 1.
6. Tolkien, J. R. R., *The Return of the King*. (New York: Random House Publishing Group. 1994), 211.
7. Excerpts from THE SILMARILLION, Second Edition by J. R. R. Tolkien, edited by Christopher Tolkien. Copyright © 1977 by J.R.R. Tolkien Copyright Trust and Christopher Reuel Tolkien. Copyright © 1981 by J. R. R. Tolkien Trust. Copyright © 1999 by Christopher Reuel Tolkien. Used by permission of Houghton Mifflin Harcourt Publishing Company. All rights reserved. 162.
8. Ibid, xv.
9. Ibid, 42.
10. Ibid, xiv.
11. Ibid, 41.
12. Ibid, 275.
13. Ibid, 40.
14. Ibid, 265.
15. Ibid, 127.

## Episode 13 / Resolution

1. Tolkien, J. R. R., *Fellowship of the Ring*. (New York: Random House Publishing Group. 1994), 65.
2. Jefferson, Thomas, excerpt inscribed on the walls of the Jefferson Memorial in the nation's capital.
3. Tolkien, J. R. R., *The Return of the King*. (New York: Random House Publishing Group. 1994), 160.

4. *The Lord of the Rings: The Return of the King,* directed by Peter Jackson (USA: New Line Cinema, 2003), Film.

## *Episode 14/ Even So*

1. Tolkien, J. R. R., *The Return of the King.* (New York: Random House Publishing Group. 1994), 290.
2. Ibid.
3. From "It Is Well With My Soul." Horatio G. Spafford. 1873. Copyright: Public Domain
4. Spiritual Thought for the Soul, *The Story of Horatio Gates Spafford.* Web. 20 December 2011. http://www.angelfire.com/ms/spiritual/page16.html

## *Episode 15 / Epilogue*

1. Shakespeare, William. "Julius Caesar." *The Complete Works of William Shakespeare.* (New York. Avenel Books. 1975), 835.
2. Wordsworth, William. "Ode: Intimations of Immortality 10." *The Norton Anthology of English Literature Vol. 2.* Ed. M. H. Abrahms. (New York: W. W. Norton & Company. 1979), 218-219.

Susan would love to hear from you.
You can reach her at:
info@silentresolveandthegodwholetmedown.com
susanvanvolkenburghbooks.wordpress.com